SAMANTABHADRA'S PRAYER

VOLUME II
With Tibetan Commentary
by Ontrul Tenpa'i Wangchuk

BY TONY DUFF
PADMA KARPO TRANSLATION COMMITTEE

Copyright © 2012 Tony Duff. All rights reserved. No portion of this book may be reproduced in any form or by any means, electronic or mechanical, including photography, recording, or by any information storage or retrieval system or technologies now known or later developed, without permission in writing from the publisher.

First edition, July 2015
ISBN paper book: 978-9937-572-83-5
ISBN e-book: 978-9937-572-82-8

Janson typeface with diacritical marks
designed and created by Tony Duff

Produced, Printed, and Published by
Padma Karpo Translation Committee
P.O. Box 4957
Kathmandu
NEPAL

Committee members for this book: translation and composition, Lama Tony Duff; sutra translation Tamás Agócs; cover design, George Romvari of Purica.

Web-site and e-mail contact through:
http://www.pktc.org/pktc
or search Padma Karpo Translation Committee on the web.

CONTENTS

VOLUME II

INTRODUCTION v
   1. The Importance of Samantabhadra's Prayer x
      1. It is one of the Five Important Prayers of the Great
         Vehicle Tradition x
      2. The Prayer's Place in Tibetan Buddhist Practice
         with a Note on its use in Dzogchen Practice in
         East Tibet xii
   2. The Origin of Samantabhadra's Prayer xiii
   3. The Prayer is an Extract xiv
      1. What are the Extracts like? xiv
      2. Problems with the Extracts xv
      3. Fixing Problems xv
   4. Explanations of the Prayer xv
      1. Indian Commentaries xvi
      2. The First Tibetan Commentary on the Prayer .. xvii
      3. Later Tibetan Commentaries on the Prayer xviii
      4. A Recent but Very Useful Tibetan Commentary . xx
      5. A Western Commentary xxi
   5. Translating the Prayer into English xxii
      1. In General xxii
      2. Specific Issues xxiii

6. Arrangement of the Materials xxvi
7. Gender Issues xxvii
8. Sanskrit xxviii
9. Supports for Study xxviii
10. Tibetan Texts xxix
11. Make a Practice Text xxix

FROM THE GAṆḌAVYŪHA SUTRA: SUDHANA MEETS WITH
THE BODHISATVA SAMANTABHADRA AND
SAMANTABHADRA EXPRESSES THE PRAYER 1

SAMANTABHADRA'S PRAYER AS ARRANGED FOR USE BY
TIBETANS 33

SAMANTABHADRA'S PRAYER AS ARRANGED FOR USE BY
NON-TIBETANS 37

A TIBETAN COMMENTARY TO SAMANTABHADRA'S PRAYER BY
ONTRUL TENPA'I WANGCHUK 43

GLOSSARY OF TERMS 157
SUPPORTS FOR STUDY 175
INDEX 181

VOLUME I

A THOROUGH EXPLANATION OF SAMANTABHADRA'S
PRAYER BY TONY DUFF

AN EXPLANATION OF SAMANTABHADRA'S PRAYER BY
NOBLE NĀGĀRJUNA

INTRODUCTION

This book is volume two in a series of books that offers, for the first time in the English language, a comprehensive guide to the prayer known as "Samantabhadra's Prayer". Note that the content of each volume, including this introduction, is exactly the same except for the commentaries that explain the prayer. This has been done so that each volume would be a complete resource, with only the explanations given in the commentaries changing. Note also that in the Tibetan tradition there are two prayers with the name "Samantabhadra's Prayer". The prayer in this series is the prayer from the Great Vehicle sutras that sets out the excellent conduct of a bodhisatva, not the prayer that explains profound Great Completion.

Samantabhadra's Prayer has been widely used by Great Vehicle Buddhists in Asia for millennia and is known to have been recited daily in Tibet by a significant portion of the Buddhist population. In recent times Western followers of Tibetan Buddhism have begun to recite translations of the prayer into English. As one of the Westerners who took up daily recital of the prayer, I sometimes recited the Tibetan text of the prayer and sometimes recited one of the translations that had been made into English. With that, I began to notice what seemed to be significant discrepancies between the existing English translations and the Tibetan text of the prayer.

During a stay in a monastery in Tibet in 2011, I was required to join a week-long all-day recitation of the prayer. Each day I saw discrepancies between the existing English translations—which I had with me—and the Tibetan version of the prayer and each day asked the head scholar of the monastery about them. His answers revealed a very high level of problems with the existing English translations. The existing translations missed many subtle but important points, had the meaning back to front or twisted around in many places, had outright mis-translations of words, had many places where the grammar had simply been ignored, and more. By the end of the week, I felt compelled to make a new English translation that would accurately reflect the wording and meaning of the prayer as understood by the tradition. I envisaged a publication that would put the new translation together with extensive explanations that would verify every wording and meaning of the prayer.

As I undertook the work, I found that there were complications surrounding the prayer, which I will now describe.

I started by assembling several Tibetan texts of the prayer and nearly twenty commentaries to it. Commentaries to it had been written in India well before the great translation of Buddhist texts into Tibetan language and several of them had been translated into Tibetan language at the time of the great translations. I obtained copies of all of them and also obtained a copy of the first commentary to the prayer written in Tibetan language, which had been written by one of the greatest of all Tibetan translators, Yeshe De, in conjunction with the Indian masters who were advising him and others during the great translations.

The first complication that I discovered was that Yeshe De's explanations of the prayer were entirely consistent with the explanations given by Indian masters in their commentaries but that, after some centuries had passed, the Tibetan "experts" writing commentaries had become so sure of their Tibetan explanations that they had stopped looking at the Indian commentaries and Yeshe De's Tibetan commentary and had started propagating their own, mistaken understandings. These misunderstandings were then passed on, everyone apparently believing what the teacher told them and no-one stopping to research the matter properly. It is obvious from looking at commentaries written over the last few centuries that their mistaken explanations have become entrenched in Tibetan explanations of the prayer. Worse, I found that those very mistakes were present in the existing English translations—the mistakes had simply been copied across from the Tibetan mistaken explanations, without further research. All in all, I found that it cannot be assumed that Tibetan commentaries of the last several centuries are correct, even if a Tibetan teacher says so. With that, I found that we non-Tibetans have to rely on Indian commentaries and Yeshe De's first Tibetan commentary to find the earliest accepted understanding of the prayer.

Next, I found that the Tibetan texts of the prayer had problems. I for one had assumed from looking at Tibetan texts of the prayer that the prayer was a standalone piece of literature formally written with a title, and so on, because the Tibetan framework that is used to package the prayer strongly conveys that sense. However, it is not a standalone prayer, rather, it is part of a sutra and the entire sutra has to be read and understood if the prayer and its wording is to be properly understood. I also found that the Tibetan framework used to package the prayer after extracting it from the sutra conveys several other things about the prayer that are not true. In short, the Tibetan framework used to package the prayer is not suitable for presenting the prayer and it is not all right to translate it from the Tibetan and use it as the framework for a translation of the prayer into other languages such as English. As a result, I had to explain all of this and make a new framework for use with translations of the prayer that would present the prayer properly.

There are other problems too, but you can begin to understand from the above why it is not a simple task to make a reliable translation of Samantabhadra's Prayer into English. Simply taking a copy of the prayer in Tibetan and translating it into English, even if done with the help of a learned Tibetan, will almost certainly result in mistakes—a reliable translation of the prayer requires much research and that has, at very least, to include a careful reading of the original sutra containing the prayer as well as multiple Indian commentaries and Yeshe De's commentary. Then, simply translating the Tibetan framework for the prayer and using that to present the prayer in English is not workable because of the faults with the Tibetan framework—a suitable framework requires the preparation of a new framework. Then, simply translating a Tibetan commentary to the prayer to explain it will probably result in mistaken explanations of the prayer in several places—to have a commentary that provides correct information requires the provision at least of an Indian commentary, an appropriate Tibetan commentary with annotations, and a commentary written directly in English. The latter is essential because the Indian and Tibetan commentaries will not cover points that need to be explained for an English translation. All of the above is what has gone into the volumes that comprise this series of books and why they form the first comprehensive and reliable presentation of Samantabhadra's Prayer to become available in English.

There is another problem, which also has to be clearly stated. The existing English translations are mistaken but, worse than that, have been used as a basis for translations of the prayer into other European languages. I know of German, French, and Russian translations made from the existing English ones and I suspect that there are more. All of these translations have been made with the assumption that the English translations are correct and will therefore provide a good basis for a translation of the prayer into another European language. Unfortunately the translators were wrong and all of these translations made from the existing English translations simply perpetuate all the mistakes of the English translations. The extent of the problem can be seen when the four or so Russian translations that are floating around the internet are considered. All of them were made on the basis of the mistaken English translations, with no reference to the original Tibetan at all. I have verified with a Russian translator that they do perpetuate all the mistakes in the English translations from which they have made. One of them trumpets its superiority over the other Russian translations by saying: "We compared four different English translations [which they listed] and made up our own version which therefore is superior to all the other existing Russian translations". In fact, their translation is even worse than the others! The translators involved did not even consider the fact that the English translations might be mistaken, let alone that blithely combining them without even looking at the Tibetan could only lead to even more mistakes!

All in all, in the two and a half thousand years since the prayer was expressed, many things have happened that conspired to cover the prayer's actual meaning. I have spoken openly about these factors that have hindered the arrival of a reliable translation of the prayer into the English and other European languages. However, this was not intended as and should not be taken as a personal attack on the Tibetan experts who have propagated mistaken explanations of the prayer. Nor was it intended as and nor should it be taken as a personal attack on the translators whose translations into English, and other European languages have been mistaken in many ways. There are various reasons why these things have happened. One worth mention is the fault of long-standing spiritual traditions in general that the people in them, in their desire to maintain the purity of the transmission, tend to blindly believe whatever the teacher or tradition says and pass that on without further investigation. That happened in Tibet where it sometimes caused significant problems with the correct transmission of meaning and it has now carried over to non-Tibetans who are trying to follow the Tibetan Buddhist ways. In this case, it has caused corruption in the presentation and explanation of the prayer of Samantabhadra. Personally, I would prefer not to talk about these problems at all, but there are people out there who want to have a reliable translation of the prayer and explanations of it so that they can use it with confidence in their own practice. For their sakes, all of this had to be explained.

1. The Importance of Samantabhadra's Prayer

1.1. It is One of the Five Important Prayers of the Great Vehicle Tradition

The Mahāyāna or Great Vehicle tradition as it came into Tibet identified five prayers as the most important ones for its followers to recite: Samantabhadra's Prayer, Mañjuśhrī's Prayer, Maitreya's Prayer, the Sukhāvatī Prayer, and the chapter of prayers in Śhāntideva's famous guide to the conduct of a bodhisatva, *Entering the Bodhisatva's Conduct*[1]. A short description of each follows.

Samantabhadra and Mañjuśhrī were the two most senior bodhisatva sons of Śhākyamuni Buddha. Both had completed the tenth bodhisatva level and were in line to become buddhas in the future. Samantabhadra, though regarded as the foremost bodhisatva of the time had been predicted to become a buddha in the far distant future[2] whereas Mañjuśhrī had been predicted to become a buddha in this era called "The Good Aeon" in which one thousand and two buddhas will appear. Regardless of the closeness or distance of their attainment of buddhahood, these two bodhisatvas were the most advanced of Śhākyamuni Buddha's bodhisatva disciples, so the prayers composed by them are particularly valuable to us who follow in their footsteps.

Maitreya's Prayer is a potent summary of the bodhisatva path and how to follow it. The prayer is generally assumed to have been composed by Maitreya who the Buddha predicted as the fifth buddha of this era, the next buddha after himself. In fact, it was

---

[1] This is the correct spelling, not "bodhisattva". See "bodhisatva" in the glossary for more information.

[2] This Samantabhadra is frequently referred to as the "bodhisatva Samantabhadra" in order to distinguish him from the primal guardian Samantabhadra of the Nyingma tantras.

composed by a previous being in the string of lives of Maitreya at a time many universes ago when that being for the first time aroused the intent to become a buddha. Padma Karpo Translation Committee has published a book containing Maitreya's Prayer, the full story of how it came about, and a commentary that clarifies its meaning.[3]

The Sukhāvatī Prayer—which is actually any of several prayers having a common purpose—has become important because it is said to create the causes for an easy exit from samsara or cyclic existence. This type of prayer creates the causes needed to leave the intermediary state following death and be born in the pure realm called Sukhāvatī of the buddha Amitābha, and so permanently escape from cyclic existence. The importance of such a prayer can be seen in the fact that Samantabhadra's Prayer includes a section which is essentially a short Sukhāvatī prayer.

The chapter of prayers in Shāntideva's *Entering the Bodhisatva's Conduct* is a distillation of prayers found in the sutras. It is so well arranged and complete that it has become popular as a liturgy for performing extensive bodhisatva prayers and also for making an extensive dedication of merit.

Samantabhadra's Prayer is regarded as the foremost of all these five major prayers and also the foremost of prayers in this era on the excellent conduct of a bodhisatva. Being foremost in those two ways is said to be a direct result of its author, Samantabhadra, being the foremost of all Shākyamuni Buddha's bodhisatva sons[4] and, in particular, the one most capable at composing prayers of aspiration for the excellent conduct of a bodhisatva. This is not mere platitude, for Samantabhadra himself says in his prayer that the prayer is "the

---

[3] *Maitreya's Sutras and Prayer with Commentary by Padma Karpo*. Publication details of all cited books are found in the supports for study section at the end of the book.

[4] See the section in this introduction about gender terminology.

best of acquisitions" for anyone in this life and that its superior qualities are due to his being the one most knowledgeable of the bodhisatva's conduct and also most capable of creating prayers of aspiration for that conduct. The commentaries to the prayer in this series explain more about this when commenting on the relevant verse towards the end of the prayer. In short, because Samantabhadra was the best in many ways at the various aspects of the Great Vehicle he had the skills needed to express what is unanimously considered to be the best of prayers of the Great Vehicle and the best of prayers on the excellent conduct of a bodhisatva.

1.2. The Prayer's Place in Tibetan Buddhist Practice with a Note on its use in Dzogchen Practice in East Tibet

Because Samantabhadra's Prayer is considered to be the best of prayers in those ways, it is very popular amongst all Tibetan practitioners—lay people, monastics, and yogins alike—and is equally popular amongst followers of all four Tibetan schools. Many Tibetans make a point of including it in their daily prayers and many also make a point of reciting large numbers of the prayer at various times during their lives.

The prayer is not only of general interest because of being regarded as the greatest of prayers in the Great Vehicle tradition, but also has a place of special importance within the various traditions of Dzogchen teachings that flourished in East Tibet during the last two and a half centuries. The Dzogchen teaching says that the approach a Dzogchen practitioner must take is described in the adage "Devotion to the guru above and compassion for sentient beings below". Thus a Dzogchen practitioner should do the core practices, which depend on devotion to guru above, and spend the rest of his time working intently on the bodhisatva's path. Therefore, Dzogchen lineages give even more importance than usual to Śāntideva's *Entering the Bodhisatva's Conduct* and Samantabhadra's Prayer. For example, there is the Dzogchen master Ontrul Tenpa'i Wangchuk who was regarded as one of the greatest Dzogchen masters alive in east Tibet until he passed away while this book was being written. His monastery in east Tibet is famous in throughout the region for its intensives in which Samantabhadra's Prayer is recited all day for several days at a time by the whole monastery—yogins, monks, nuns, and lay people alike. In that practice, the assembly does not merely recite the prayer but recites it within the context of an extensive liturgy that neatly and beautifully wraps the recitation of the prayer into a full day of complete Great Vehicle practice. I have, as mentioned earlier, done one of these intensives. At the time, Ontrul Tenpa'i Wangchuk encouraged me to translate the liturgy into English and it is my hope to bring the tradition of day-long recitations of Samantabhadra's Prayer, done with the liturgy, to the West.

2. The Origin of Samantabhadra's Prayer

It is often thought that Samantabhadra's Prayer is a standalone prayer made for general use, but that is not so. It is the conclusion, composed in verse, to a teaching on the conduct of a bodhisatva that was given to a young bodhisatva named Sudhana when he encountered the tenth-level bodhisatva Samantabhadra. The entire story with the teaching and concluding verses was written down in detail in the last chapter of a large sutra of the Great Vehicle named the *Gaṇḍavyūha Sutra*, which in turn is the last sutra of an extremely large collection of Great Vehicle sutras called the *Avataṃsaka Sutra*.

In order to understand the verses and to be able to recite them while realizing the full significance of their words, it is essential to have read that chapter and some explanation at least of its very profound meaning. To assist with that, we have translated the chapter into English in this book and provided a brief explanation of it in the commentary to the prayer by myself in volume one.

It has to be emphasized that knowing the story of the verses is essential to being able to understand and use the verses as a prayer. When the verses are recited without having read and thought about the story behind them, an important part of their meaning, and with that their potency, is lost. For example, Samantabhadra frequently speaks of beyond-ordinary levels of experience in the verses and these are not mere concepts that he is adding to embellish them but are direct expressions of his own, master of the tenth bodhisatva level, state of being. Therefore, someone who first reads and thinks about the story behind the verses will understand the intent of the verses and will also have opened the door to connecting directly with that state of being, making the recitation of the verses as a prayer more potent in every way. You are urged to go now to that chapter on page 1 and read it.

3. The Prayer is an Extract

The sutra with the meeting of Sudhana and Samantabhadra plus the verses is too long to use for recitation. However, the concluding verses are very suited to the purpose. Therefore, at some point in ancient India the verses alone were extracted from the sutra and written down separately for use as a prayer for recitation. The same thing was done later on in Tibet.

3.1. What are the Extracts Like?

Indian Buddhists extracted the verses from the sutra and wrote them down in a very simple format—they wrote the name "Samantabhadra's Prayer" followed by the verses. Later, when the Tibetans first translated the sutra, they did the same, using the same simple arrangement as the Indians. However, the Tibetans later shifted to a complicated arrangement that packed the verses into a framework that had been royally decreed as the framework for holding all such translations. That arrangement of the verses within that framework has been in use for over one thousand years. It has sometimes been corrupted during that time, but the basic and most commonly seen form of it can be seen, translated into English, on page 33.

3.2. Problems with the Extracts

The extracts just described are convenient for personal use. However, there is nothing about them that says that the verses in them are an integral and important part of something larger. Instead, the extracts lead people to believe that the verses are a standalone prayer with no relation to anything else. Then those people never know about the all-important context of the verses, with the result that their full import is lost.

The complicated Tibetan arrangement has that and several other problems with it. Most translations of the prayer into English have simply translated the entire Tibetan extract, carrying all of these problems into English. Therefore, if you are using one of those English translations, it is important to know about these problems. The details are clearly explained in my Thorough Explanation to Samantabhadra's Prayer in volume one of this series.

3.3. Fixing the Problems

It is not hard to fix the problems with the problematic Tibetan arrangement. All that is needed is to make a revised framework that correctly informs the reader of the original context of the prayer and provides the reader with other, correct information. I have made such a framework for English, but the same framework could and I hope will be used for other languages. It can be seen on page 37.

4. Explanations of the Prayer

In the short space of sixty-two four-line verses, the prayer covers many of the key points of the Great Vehicle teaching. As a result, there are many places where the literal meaning of the words might seem obvious but their full import can only be known through a careful explanation of the relevant points of the Great Vehicle teaching. Moreover, there are many places where the prayer is so terse that even the literal meaning cannot be known without further explanation. And still further, there are many places where the Sanskrit syntax of the original prayer has to be correctly understood in order to understand the syntax of the prayer and also to see the fullness of the meaning cleverly woven into the expression of the prayer. Finally, there are points of grammar in the composition of the prayer which need to be clarified. Altogether, the prayer needs a significant amount of explanation to be correctly understood, so, what explanations are available to us?

4.1. Indian Commentaries

The earliest explanations that I have seen are in commentaries composed by Indian masters, starting with Nāgārjuna. Several of them were translated and preserved by the Tibetans in their *Translated Treatises*[5] at the time of the great translations in Tibet. The earliest is an oral teaching given by master Nāgārjuna [100 C.E.][6] that was recorded in writing by one of his students. After that there were commentaries composed in writing by the masters Shākyamitra, a heart disciple of Nāgārjuna, Vasubhandu [375–430], Dignāga [480–540], and Bhadravaha.

I read all of those Indian commentaries. It was obvious from doing so that there was a strong commentarial tradition in India on which these masters agreed. Moreover, bearing in mind that the original Sanskrit language of the prayer was the native language of these masters, it was clear that they knew the points in the prayer where the language of the prayer had to be explained. These points made all the commentaries of special value not only for understanding the prayer but for translating it too.

---

[5] For *Translated Treatises*, see the glossary.

[6] There are questions about the dates of Nāgārjuna. However, his commentary seems to have preceded all the others, and the earliest date given for him, the one given here, seems to be appropriate.

I found that master Nāgārjuna's commentary was especially useful. His explanations not only had the mark of an expert who could explain the meaning of the words according to the Great Vehicle tradition but also had the mark of a supreme expert who, knowing the points at which misunderstanding could arise, made a point of definitively stating the meaning at those points. I found his commentary to be essential reading for obtaining an accurate understanding of what the verses of the prayer actually say. Additionally, I found it to be the best basis for translators needing a commentary that would elucidate every aspect of the prayer according to the language in which it was originally composed—its literal meaning, syntax, and grammar.

These Indian commentaries, and especially Nāgārjuna's commentary, were the basis for the official translation of the prayer into the Tibetan language and, having read them, I am sure must also be the basis for translations into languages other than Tibetan.

4.2. The First Tibetan Commentary on the Prayer

The first Tibetan commentary to the verses was composed by the great translator Yeshe De. He was the chief translator of many sutras, including the *Gaṇḍavyūha Sutra* containing the verses of Samantabhadra's Prayer, at the time of the great translations in Tibet. It is important to note that he was considered to be one of the three greatest translators during that period and was famed for his vast knowledge of scripture, Sanskrit, and how to translate Sanskrit into Tibetan.

In order to translate Samantabhadra's Prayer from Sanskrit into Tibetan, he relied on the Indian commentaries mentioned just above and also received explanations in person from the Indian masters who were advising him at the time. He incorporated all of this knowledge into one of the largest Tibetan commentaries on the prayer that has ever been written. I found that his commentary agreed with the Indian commentaries and also included many explanations of how the Sanskrit should be understood in Tibetan. As expected, his commentary had the same uncluttered style as the Indian commentaries in which there is simply commentary on the verses and none of the artificiality seen in later Tibetan commentaries that comes with explaining the Tibetan framework for the extracted verses.

Yeshe De's commentary also has to be set, together with Nāgārjuna's commentary and other Indian commentaries, as the basis for translations of the prayer from Tibetan into languages other than Tibetan.

4.3. Later Tibetan Commentaries on the Prayer

As time went by, a number of commentaries to the prayer were written by Tibetan experts. Unfortunately, several centuries ago—I have not been able to pin down exactly when, but four hundred or more years ago—it seems that these "experts" stopped going back to the Indian commentaries and to Yeshe De's commentary written based on the explanations of Indian experts. As a result, mistakes began to arise in the Tibetan way of explaining and hence commenting on the verses.

The Tibetan commentaries most commonly mentioned or used these days are now discussed. There is a commentary by each of two of the hierarchs of the Jonang lineage—the famous Tāranātha [1575–1634] and Tobbar Ozer—but both commentaries impose a structure on the prayer which is not found in any other commentary and which has been called into question by other Tibetan masters.

Followers of Kagyu and Nyingma schools of Tibetan Buddhism often rely on the commentary of Karma Chagmey Raga Asyas [1613–1679], a great Kagyu master who had close ties to the Nyingma tradition. His commentary is short and sometimes a little unclear because of its brevity. Nevertheless, it has been popular because it is easy to read. With his commentary, we can see that, by the seventeenth century C.E., mis-understandings of Sanskrit syntax and grammar have crept into commentaries on the prayer. From that time on, we find that all Tibetan commentaries on the prayer simply repeat the mistakes.

Tibetans generally accept that Lochen Dharmashrī[7] of Mindroling monastery [1654–1717] was one of the greatest Tibetan translators in more recent times. He was reputed to have a vast knowledge of Sanskrit and his translations and statements about translations are generally regarded as infallible. Therefore, it was very surprising to find that his commentary on Samantabhadra's Prayer also shows the failure to understand Sanskrit syntax that was mentioned in an earlier section, making his commentary less than reliable.

Shortly after Lochen Dharmashrī wrote his commentary, the exceptionally knowledgeable Gelugpa master Changkya Rolpa'i Dorje [1717–1786] wrote a commentary to the prayer. His commentary is especially favoured by followers of the Gelugpa school.

A small commentary written in recent times by a Tibetan hermit who was a follower of the Khyentse lineage has to be mentioned because it was translated into English then widely distributed amongst Western practitioners who have been using it since then. This is really unfortunate because the Tibetan commentary is mistaken in many places and the translation into English not only embodies those mistakes but also has many other mistakes in it. The commentary was published in the early 1980's under the name of the Marpa Translation Committee, with the name of Elizabeth Callahan mentioned as the translator of the commentary. A copy of the prayer based on this translation has been widely distributed in the West. It is one of the English translations that I found to have significant problems. Unfortunately, it has been used as a basis for translations into other European languages, thereby propagating the errors.

---

[7] "Lochen" means "great translator".

My conclusion is the later Tibetan commentaries do not have anything special to commend them over the commentaries of the Indian masters and Yeshe De. At very least, these later Tibetan commentaries have to be read and their content understood in relation to those earlier commentaries.

4.4. A Recent but Very Useful Tibetan Commentary

For the sake of completeness, a Tibetan commentary needs to be included in this series. I chose a very recent one by the great Tibetan master Ontrul Tenpa'i Wangchuk who was mentioned earlier in this commentary. Tenpa'i Wangchuk was an unusually good scholar and a great Dzogchen master. His commentary to the prayer was given as an oral teaching to the lay men and women yogis living in his encampment that was then written down and included in his collected works.

His commentary has two distinct features that make it a particularly useful resource for the reader. Firstly, it is far more detailed and hence longer than any of the other commentaries mentioned so far. It goes through the meaning of the words of the verses in great detail, giving explanations that leave nothing un-examined. Secondly, it stays focussed on explaining the prayer in a very practical way and does not go off into scholarly investigations. It is unique in that last respect, being the only commentary to the prayer that I know of that shows the prayer in a very practical light. English-speaking practitioners who recite the prayer regularly will find it to be a treasure-trove of instruction.

His commentary is what is called a "bitwise" commentary; it quotes a word or a phrase or perhaps a chunk of the prayer then explains that "bit" of the prayer. A bit-wise commentary allows the exact meaning of the words of the prayer to be easily understood and in a way that allows no room for doubt. The "bits" of the prayer being commented on are marked off in the Tibetan text and that has been carried over into the English translation by marking them off in bold italics. In e-book versions, they are additionally given a different colour from the rest of the text, making them even easier to see.

The lineage of the commentary also is very interesting. It comes from the masters of the relatively-recent Longchen Nyingthig lineage of the Dzogchen teaching, a lineage that began in the late 1700's with Jigmey Lingpa and flourished greatly in Eastern Tibet. One of the early masters of the system was the very learned and highly accomplished Dza Patrul [1808-1887] who spent most of his life at Dzogchen Monastery in East Tibet. Dza Patrul gave oral instructions on the prayer that were preserved in a verbal transmission and not committed to paper until Adzom Gyalsay [1842–1924] recorded them in writing. From there, the oral tradition for this commentary came down from Adzom Gyalsay to Lodro Gyatso of Dzogchen Monastery [?–2003]—a master who died a few years before this book was written and who at the time of his passing showed all the signs of having achieved buddhahood in his very life. It was given to him to his heart disciple, Ontrul Tenpa'i Wangchuk who passed away while this book was being written.

Ontrul Tenpa'i Wangchuk was an extraordinary scholar as well as great master of Dzogchen, and his commentaries in general have become famous amongst Tibetans around the world for their in-depth yet very practical style. As a matter of good fortune, while receiving his complete teachings in Tibet in 2011, I received the complete reading transmission for this commentary together with all of his other works and was then encouraged by him to translate all of them.

4.5. A Western Commentary

There is a mass of detail that comes from that reading all those Indian and Tibetan commentaries that has to be drawn together in place. As well as that, there are many points of English grammar, syntax, and meaning connected with the prayer that are not covered in the Indian and Tibetan commentaries and could only be covered in a commentary written directly in English. Therefore, I wrote a very extensive commentary that brought all of this information together in one place. You will find that it will clarify many points about the prayer.

5. Translating the Prayer into English

5.1. In general

The best way to translate the prayer would be to do what the Tibetans did—to translate the entire *Gaṇḍavyūha Sutra* or at least its chapter with the entire story of Sudhana's meeting with Samantabhadra and then simply extract the verses into a suitable framework for the prayer. Translating the entire sutra was more than could be done here, so it was decided to translate the entire chapter with the story of the meeting.

An original Sanskrit version would be the best source for such a translation but is not available, so I had to rely on the translations that had been made into Tibetan or Chinese. The Chinese version of the sutra has already been translated into English by Thomas Cleary, but the Tibetan version is closer to the original Sanskrit for linguistic reasons and hence better suited as a basis for translation into other languages, therefore I used that.

The Tibetan translation of the *Gaṇḍavyūha Sutra* is preserved in *The Translated Word*. There are seven major editions of *The Translated Word* of which the Derge edition is, for various reasons, regarded as excellent, so I settled on that. In particular, I used a recently-published comparative edition of *The Translated Word*, one that presents the Derge edition but with every difference between it and the other six editions carefully noted. I found that there were differences in the Tibetan wording of the verses between the seven editions, most of which were slight and did not end up affecting the meaning as it would be translated into English, but a few of which were major and could not be reconciled. After looking at the differences involved, I saw that to make a critical edition of the prayer in English would result in an extremely complex translation that would not be usable by practitioners who are, in the end, the audience for whom this book and its translations are intended. Therefore the Derge edition's reading of the prayer was set as the basis for the translation into English.

The chapter to be translated is, starting at the beginning of the meeting between Sudhana and Samantabhadra and going down to the beginning of the verses at the very end of the sutra, straightforward if one is well-versed in the Great Vehicle sutras. However, the verses need explanation and I have stated above which sources are best for those explanations.

5.2. Specific Issues

This section presents some specific issues related to the translation of the verses of the prayer.

5.2.1. Added verses

The official Tibetan translation of the verses of the prayer found in all editions of the *Translated Word* is comprised of sixty-two verses. However, it is probable that the sixty-first and sixty-second verses were not part of the original but were added in India before the sutra came to Tibet. The earlier Indian commentaries do not mention the sixty-first and sixty-second two verses, for example, Nāgārjuna's commentary abruptly ends following the explanation of the sixtieth verse. Then, Yeshe De says that the Indian masters advising him acknowledged that the sixty-first and second verses were probably Indian additions, but in the end advised him to keep the two verses in the official translation of the prayer into Tibetan. Thus, the actual number of verses in the original prayer cannot be known with certainty, but there is a strong probability that the sixty-first and sixty-second verses as are not part of the original.

On top of that, when the Tibetans extracted the sixty-two verses from the sutra in the *Translated Word* into their framework as described earlier, they added a verse composed by the great Tibetan translator Vairochana to the end of the official translation. Thus, the Tibetan texts of the prayer came to have sixty-three verses. You can see this verse in the Tibetan framework on page 33. It is not part of the prayer and should not be made part of English translations of the prayer.

5.2.2. Misunderstandings of Sanskrit syntax

Having read all the Indian commentaries and then Yeshe De's commentary, I believe that Yeshe De translated the prayer into Tibetan well. His commentary, as can be seen from reading the available Indian commentaries translated into Tibetan, presents the Indian understanding of the syntax of the prayer as originally written in Sanskrit. However, some centuries ago, Tibetans experts began to write commentaries in which they incorrectly explained some places in the prayer due to incorrectly understanding certain Sanskrit constructions that had been correctly translated by Yeshe De into Tibetan. All currently-available English translations and translations into other European languages that I know of have inherited this type of mistake.

A clear example of this type of mistake can be seen in the explanation of the very first words of the first verse of the prayer given in Tibetan commentaries of the last several centuries. A full explanation of this appears in my Thorough Explanation of Samantabhadra's Prayer in volume one of the series. Other mistakes of this type have appeared in Tibetan commentaries and they too are fully explained in my Thorough Explanation.

5.2.3. Misunderstandings of words

From the foregoing, we know that this is a prayer spoken by a master of the tenth bodhisatva level, which means that it was spoken by someone with an amazing capacity for expressing the teaching in words. The prayer is a masterpiece of composition and, with that, has an exceptional level of meaning packed into a very short space. As a result, it is very easy to mistake the meaning of the words of the prayer.

Tibetan commentaries mostly explain the words of the prayer correctly, though later ones sometimes have mistakes at that level. Existing English translations on the other hand, because it seems of lack of familiarity with the vocabulary, with the details of the vast teachings of the Great Vehicle, and especially with the details of Tibetan grammar, have many mistakes.

5.2.4. Discrepancies between wordings of the verses

It would have been very nice if the verses as they appear in the sutra and in the arrangements for its use as a prayer and in the commentaries on the verses all used exactly the same wording of the verses, but they do not. The differences are often small and in many cases do not change the rendering in English. However, sometimes it is not so.

As mentioned above, I first produced a translation of the verses into English based on the official Tibetan translation as it appears in the Derge edition of *The Translated Word*. That is the version intended for readers to use as the basis for keeping, reciting, and teaching the prayer. After that, rather than try to force that to be consistent with what is in the commentaries and the texts of the prayer, I simply translated them as is.

This lack of consistency can be very frustrating to all of us who would like to see an exact match between the verses as they appear in the sutra, in the commentaries, and texts of the prayer. However, we have reached a time when we have to accept that translations of our beloved Buddhist literature cannot always be done perfectly. It is a sign of our degenerate times.

6. Arrangement of the Materials

There is a deliberate order to the various materials presented in the books comprising this series. This introduction comes first to lay the ground. Then the main part of each book begins with the complete record of Sudhana and Samantabhadra's meeting as found in the *Gaṇḍavyūha Sutra*. It is placed first because, as explained earlier, Samantabhadra's Prayer is an integral part of the sutra and the sutra must be read first to gain a proper understanding of the verses that form Samantabhadra's Prayer.

The sutra with the verses of the prayer is followed by the framework used to contain the verses when they have been extracted from the sutra for use as a prayer. First there is the Tibetan framework then there is the new framework I have made in order to overcome the many problems with the Tibetan framework. Both have been explained in this introduction and further explanations of them are available in my own commentary in volume one.

Once the original form of the prayer then the frameworks used to contain it have been seen and understood, the reader needs to have clear explanations of the many difficult points of the prayer. Therefore, each volume then contains one or more commentaries to explain the prayer thoroughly. At the moment there are three commentaries in two volumes of the series—one each by an Indian, Tibetan, and English-speaking expert. Of them, my commentary written directly in English is placed first in volume one because it gives most clarification of the prayer. The terse Indian commentary by Nāgārjuna follows it. Then the very long and highly practical Tibetan commentary by Tenpa'i Wangchuk appears in the second volume. The commentaries can be read alone but reading them in conjunction with one another brings significant rewards.

7. Gender Issues

The ideas about human gender in ancient India and Tibet were very different from today's Western ideas of it. However, that does not give us the right to blithely change the wording of texts written in those cultures and times to suit ourselves. This book translates materials from those cultures and times and in doing so presents what those materials are saying, not someone's opinion—often emotionally charged—about what they should say.

If those who do not like this approach were to take the time to study in depth the meanings transmitted with for example wordings like "bodhisatva sons" or "sons of the conqueror", they would find that this is not mere exclusion of women, but that the words support an enormous amount of carefully thought out teaching. For example, the bodhisatva teachings speak of buddha "sons" because they are the ones who carry on the line of the tathāgatas. There is a thread to that that runs through the entirety of the Buddha's teaching and is lost if the translation is changed. If you have a extensive knowledge of the Buddha's teachings, you will understand this point and have no trouble with it, regardless of your status as man or woman. This use of "sons" is not intended to exclude women and in fact, because of its usage, both men and women are included.

I could write here extensively on this point but I see little value to it. The fact is that the materials being translated use gender terms and it is not my job or anyone else's job to change them and lose important threads of meaning in the process. Of course, if you use the prayer for recitation and want to change the gender wording to suit yourself, you are free to go ahead and do so. It seems to me that that is the correct solution to what has become a problem for some people, not the solution of insisting that translators change the wording of ancient texts to suit others' emotional needs.

8. Sanskrit

Sanskrit terms are an important aspect of a technical book like this. They are properly rendered into English with diacritical marks. For the sake of precision, diacritical marks have been used with them throughout this book.

The IATS system of transliteration of Sanskrit, which is the one generally in use in academic circles is hard for non-scholars to read. Therefore, we have modified that system slightly to make the transliterated Sanskrit more readable even when the meaning of the diacritical marks is not understood. This same approach seems to becoming commonplace amongst translators of Tibetan Buddhism. In it:

> ś is written the way it sounds, as śh ;
> ṣ is written similarly as ṣh ; and
> ṛ is written similarly as ṛi ;
> ca is written as cha;
> cha is written as chha.

The other letters for transliteration are used in the same way as they are used in the IATS scheme. In general, if you do not understand the system, simply read the letters as though they did not have the diacritical marks and, with our modified system, you will have a good approximation to the actual pronunciation.

9. Supports for Study

Padma Karpo Translation Committee has amassed a range of materials to help those who are studying this and related topics. In particular several books on sutras have been published, all of which support each other and each of which clarifies another important aspect of the Buddhist teaching. Please see the chapter Supports for Study at the end of the book for the details.

10. Tibetan Texts

We make a point of publishing the Tibetan texts together with the English translations where possible. Space considerations meant that it was not possible with this book. However, a complete set of the Tibetan texts for this book have been made available for free in digital format on our PKTC web-site.

11. Make a Practice Text

If you would like a text of the prayer for practice, you could make a copy of the framework for the prayer on page 37, then copy the prayer out of the sutra and add it into the framework at the place marked in the framework. The prayer in the sutra starts on page 23. There will also be a free edition of the prayer set up as a practice text for recitation on our PKTC web-site.

Tony Duff,
Swayambunath,
Nepal,
June, 2015

From the Great Vehicle Gandavyuha Sutra:

Sudhana's Meeting with the Bodhisatva Samantabhadra Culminating in Samantabhdra's Prayer

What follows is taken from the final section of the last chapter of the Great Vehicle *Gaṇḍavyūha Sutra*. In it, Sudhana meets with the great bodhisatva Samantabhadra who teaches him then sums up all that has happened in the meeting by expressing it clearly in verse.

The translation was made from the *Gaṇḍvyūha Sutra* as found in a reprint of the blocks of the Derge Black edition of *The Translated Word* published in Chengdu, China in the 1990's. A scanned copy of the reprint downloaded from the Tibetan Buddhist Resource Center, TBRC Volume Number 923, TBRC Work Number 22084 was used. Page and line numbers are incorporated into the English text for the use of those who want to follow the Tibetan.

———— ◆◆◆ ————

The twenty-second bundle.[8]

689.2 Then, the merchant's son Sudhana—who had respectfully apprenticed with spiritual friends as numerous as the extremely subtle atoms of a great third-order thousandfold world realm; who possessed a mind in which the accumulations for all-knowingness had been gathered; who had engaged in, by keeping in harmony with, the oral instructions and teachings of all spiritual friends; who had gone with the same thought to the feet of all spiritual friends; who possessed a mind which understood that all spiritual friends are, because they are to be pleased, not to be displeased; who had followed the ocean-like oral instruction and teaching of all spiritual

---

[8] Sanskrit texts were written on palm leaves which were then stitched together in bundles. The original Sanskrit edition of the *Gaṇḍvyūha Sutra* that was used as a basis for the Tibetan translation came in a set of twenty-two bundles. Translations of sutras into Tibetan usually recorded the number of each Sanskrit bundle, as was done here.

friends; who possessed an essence which was genuinely arisen from the ocean-like thought of great compassion; who had completely brightened all migrators with a cloud of the varieties of great loving kindness; who possessed a body in which a force of great joy had been highly developed; who lived in utter peace within the vast complete emancipation of a bodhisatva; who possessed the eye of giving due to giving that strongly came forth from every possible door; who had utterly completed a careful development of the ocean-like good qualities of all tathāgatas; who had entered into the path which is the one that all tathāgatas admire; who had completely developed the force of perseverance needed for the accumulation of all-knowingness; who possessed a mind that had been thoroughly processed using the minds and thoughts of all bodhisatvas; who had engaged in a stream one after another all of the tathāgatas of the three times[9]; **690** who had mastered the ocean-like modes of dharma of all the buddhas; who had followed the ocean-like wheels of all the tathāgatas; who possessed a domain such that he could wholly show his image in all the world's birthplaces; who had entered into the ocean of varieties of prayer of all bodhisatvas; who had utterly entered into the bodhisatva conduct for all aeons; who had utterly gained the appearance of the objects of all-knowingness; who had completely developed all of the bodhisatva faculties; who had utterly gained the appearances of the path of all-knowingness; who had appearances without obscuration in all directions; who possessed a mind which had utterly entered all modes of dharmadhātus; who had utterly accomplished appearance in all modes of fields; who had gone into, in a way without discordance with their mindstreams, working for the sake of all the infinite sentient beings; who had completely destroyed all the mountains of abysmal obscuration; who had followed the dharma which is without obscuration; who had thoroughly assessed in utter peace the bodhisatva's complete

---

[9] This refers to what is spoken of later in the prayer, a bodhisatva's development of the capacity to step through the buddha-fields of all of the buddhas, one after another, meeting the buddhas of all of those fields, one after another.

emancipation having an essence of dharmadhātu present as the ground of all levels; who had sought out the domain of all tathāgatas; and who had been blessed by all tathāgatas—completely assessed[10] and became present in the domain of the bodhisatva Samantabhadra.

Then, having heard the name of the bodhisatva mahāsatva Samantabhadra, heard of his bodhisatva conduct, heard of his special prayers, heard of his special engagement in and remaining within the entire accomplishment of accumulation, heard of his special path of attainment and occurrence, **691** heard of the mindstream connected with the mode of Samantabhadra's level, heard of the accumulation connected with the level, heard of the force connected with the gaining of the level, heard of his wholly treading upon the level, heard of his abiding on the level, heard of his treading upon it by casting off the previous level, heard of the level's domain, heard of the level's blessing, and heard of his truly abiding on the level, he was glad at the prospect and eager to see the bodhisatva Samantabhadra w—his mind of extreme openness like the expanse of space was elevated above all clinging, and the perception of a field was something he had meditated on in the extreme, and his mind of true transcendence over all possibility of being affected had a domain which was without obscuration for all dharmas, and his mind of being without impediment extensively filled all the direction-oceans, and his mind of being without obscuration entirely trod the objects of all-knowingness, and his mind of extreme complete purity had entirely purified the core, the enlightenment ornament, by vipaśhyanā, and his mind of having made extreme classifications had entered the dharma ocean of all the buddhas, and his mind of extreme vastness was to thoroughly ripen sentient beings of all makeups, and his mind of extensively filling and highly distinguishing taming was doing the entire purification of all buddha-fields, and his mind of measurelessness was going forth as an image into the

---

[10] "Completely assessed" means that he had entered into Samantabhadra's domain, carefully taken note of all of its particulars and was, in that way, fully present there.

maṇḍala of the retinue of every buddha, and his mind which because of remaining throughout all aeons had no end and was without final limit was not fearful of the strength of all the tathāgatas, and because of the final limit of the unmixed buddha-dharmas he was one who had the core enlightenment present as the vajra holy core. He was seated on a lotus seat a mound of all kinds of jewels, with the tathāgata's seat, a lion-throne, in view directly ahead of him.

Then, the merchant's son Sudhana, **692** because of being moist with roots of virtue from the past that came from diligently pursuing intentions and ideas of that sort, having the blessing of all tathāgatas, and having a karmic lot of roots of virtue from the past consistent with that of the bodhisatva Samantabhadra, ten portents arose indicating that he would see the bodhisatva Samantabhadra. What were the ten? They were as follows. All buddha-fields became complete purity through the complete purity of the core of all tathāgatas, the enlightenment ornament. All buddha-fields became complete purity through all unfree states and bad migrations and paths to bad migrations being completely removed. All buddha-fields became complete purity, as with a lotus-grove's ornament, through the complete purity of a buddha-field. All buddha-fields became complete purity through making all sentient beings' body and mind glad and content. All buddha-fields became complete purity through ever remaining in the nature of all jewels. All buddha-fields became complete purity through sentient beings of all makeups always remaining in being utterly ornamented by the excellent marks and signs. All buddha-fields became complete purity through always remaining in being totally covered by clouds that adorn and move about. All buddha-fields became complete purity through sentient beings of all makeups always remaining in the possession of minds of mutual loving kindness, mutual benefit, and mutual being without malicious mind. All buddha-fields became complete purity through always remaining in being ornamented by the core, the enlightenment ornament. All buddha-fields became complete purity through all sentient beings always remaining in diligently thinking of the recollection of buddha. **693** Those were the ten portents that arose indicating that he would see the bodhisatva mahāsatva Samantabhadra.

Furthermore, ten great appearance portents arose indicating that he would see the bodhisatva mahāsatva Samantabhadra. What were the ten? They were as follows. From the extremely subtle atoms of all world realms and moreover from each extremely subtle atom, many nets of light-rays of all the tathāgatas became completely apparent. From the extremely subtle atoms of all world realms, moreover from each extremely subtle atom, many light mandalas of all the buddhas issued forth—in one colour, in various colours, and in many hundreds of thousands of colours, extensively filling all dharmadhātus. From the extremely subtle atoms of all world realms, moreover from each extremely subtle atom, clouds of all kinds of jewels showing up many shapes of all the tathāgatas issued forth, extensively filling all dharmadhātus. From the extremely subtle atoms of all world realms, moreover from each extremely subtle atom, many clouds of wheels and mandalas of the radiant light of all the tathāgatas issued forth, extensively filling all dharmadhātus. From the extremely subtle atoms of all world realms, moreover from each extremely subtle atom, many clouds of aromatic substances, flowers, garlands, ointments, and incenses issued forth, resounding with thunder of all the clouds of the ocean-like dharmas of the good qualities of the bodhisatva Samantabhadra and extensively filling all dharmadhātus of the ten directions. **694** From the extremely subtle atoms of all world realms, moreover from each extremely subtle atom, many clouds of suns and moons and stars issued forth, utterly giving off the light of bodhisatva Samantabhadra and extensively filling all dharmadhātus. From the extremely subtle atoms of all world realms, moreover from each extremely subtle atom, many clouds of oil-lamps present as all the shapes of bodies issued forth, utterly illuminating like the light-rays of a buddha and extensively filling all dharmadhātus. From the extremely subtle atoms of all world realms, moreover from each extremely subtle atom, many clouds of precious gem-forms, appearing as the bodies of all the tathāgatas, issued forth, extensively filling all world realms of the ten directions. From the extremely subtle atoms of all world realms, moreover from each extremely subtle atom, many clouds of light-forms appearing in the shape of the bodies of all the tathāgatas issued forth; a rain of clouds of the blessings and prayers of all buddhas strongly fell and all dharmadhatus were extensively filled. From the extremely subtle atoms of all world realms, moreover from each extremely subtle atom, a cloud ocean with all the types of forms of bodies of bodhisatvas appearing as colour images, and they, possessing the yogas for rescuing all beings, performing many completions of the dharma thoughts of all sentient beings, issued forth, extensively filling all dharmadhātus. Those were the ten great appearance portents that arose indicating that he would see the bodhisatva mahāsatva Samantabhadra. **695**

Then, the merchant's son Sudhana having seen those ten appearances which were portents, the occasion during which he would see the bodhisatva Samantabhadra began—his own roots of virtue had supported it; all of the tathāgatas had blessed it; the appearance of the dharma of all the tathāgatas actually occurred; the conduct of bodhisatva Samantabhadra became manifest; the bodhisatva Samantabhadra, through the blessing contained in his prayer, blessed it; in the domain of all tathāgatas, it was truly admired; the strength and force of extreme certainty about the tremendous domain of a bodhisatva was utterly gained; he was thinking that if he saw the bodhisatva Samantabhadra, it would be equivalent to attaining all-knowingness; the faculty for being able to see the bodhisatva Samantabhadra became manifest; a great force of perseverance for being able to see the bodhisatva Samantabhadra was gained; a yoga of irreversible perseverance in seeking out the bodhisatva Samantabhadra came into his possession; with a bodhisatva-body that could tread everywhere by a sphere of sense faculties manifest throughout all directions and concomitant total viewing and a mind to follow after bodhisatva Samantabhadra who was present at the feet of all buddhas without exception he was truly given to the observation of all tathāgatas, and he was minding not to separate from seeking observation of the bodhisatva Samantabhadra, and with his eye of wisdom having at core the idea that he should observe the bodhisatva Samantabhada he had entered the path of the bodhisatva Samantabhadra, **696** and he had an intention vast as the expanse of space, and a special intention of wielding the vajra of great compassion, and aspired to follow after the bodhisatva Samantabhadra, and was blessed until the end of the final aeon of the future, and had a completely pure ability to tread everywhere[11], and went into conduct the same as the bodhisatva Samantabhadra's conduct, and came to dwell in the wisdom of abiding on the level of the bodhisatva Samantabhadra, and came into the possession of truly abiding in the place of all tathāgatas. He saw the bodhisatva Samantabhadra—who had attained sameness with all the tathāgatas, had gone to three times sameness, had come into possession of an inconceivable place, had a domain he could not be deprived of, had come to possess a place of boundless wisdom, would be fully viewed by all bodhisatvas, could not be overcome by anyone in the world, would be followed by all the retinue-maṇḍalas, and come into possession of a truly elevated body—he saw him seated in direct view of the bhagavan tathāgata Vairochana in the maṇḍala-ocean of the bodhisatva retinue, totally surrounded by a bodhisatva assembly, seated in front of the bodhisatva saṅgha, and sitting on a precious lion-throne with heart of a great lotus.

He saw many clouds of light-rays numbering the extremely subtle atoms of all buddha fields issue forth from every one of the hairs from all his hair-pores which then utterly illuminated all the world realms infinite as the dharmadhātu reaching to the limits of space then were pacifying the suffering of sentient beings. **697** He saw maṇḍalas of light, many clouds having a variety of colours, numbering the extremely subtle atoms of all buddha fields issue forth from his body, which were vastly increasing the force of all bodhisatvas' joy and admiration. He saw many rains present in a variety of colours of clouds of aromatic substance-radiant-light, strongly issue

---

[11] ... meaning that his capacity for treading through aeons of time to their limit and through buddha-fields with their buddhas and bodhisatva sons to their limit was truly perfected ...

forth from his crown, his two shoulder bumps, and all of his hairs, which extensively filled the retinue-mandalas of all the tathāgatas, strongly coming down. He saw many rains, numerous as the extremely subtle atoms of all buddha-fields, of clouds of all kinds of flowers strongly issue forth from each and every hair from all his hair-pores, which extensively filled the retinue-maṇḍalas of all the tathāgatas, strongly pouring down. He saw many clouds of trees of various aromatic substances, numerous as the extremely subtle atoms of all buddha-fields, strongly issue forth from each and every hair from all his hair-pores, which extensively filled all dharmadhātus infinite as the limits of the expanses of space, adorned them with the ornament of clouds of trees of aromatic substances which utterly sent out a rain of an inexhaustible store of aromatic substances, powders, and incense and extensively filled the retinue-mandalas of all the tathāgatas, strongly pouring down. He saw many clouds of various clothes strongly issue forth from each and every hair from all his hair-pores, totally clothing and so adorning all dharmadhātus, infinite as the limits of the expanse of space. He saw a rain of clouds of shawls of various silks, of clouds of various garlands, and of clouds of various pearls, and clouds of wish-fulfilling precious gems **698** numerous as the extremely subtle atoms of all buddha-fields strongly issue forth from each and every hair from all his hair-pores, which extensively filled the retinue-maṇḍalas of all the tathāgatas, strongly pouring down. He saw clouds of jewel trees numerous as the extremely subtle atoms of all buddha-fields strongly issue forth from each and every hair from all his hair-pores for the purpose of completely fulfilling the thoughts of all sentient beings extensively fill all dharmadhātus infinite as the limits of the expanse of space, then ornament them with ornamentation radiated from the precious trees in the form of a store of jewels, making a great rain of jewels strongly fall in the retinue-mandalas of all the tathāgatas. He saw clouds of the strata of the form-realm gods numerous as the extremely subtle atoms of all buddha-fields strongly issue forth from each and every hair from all his hair-pores, giving genuine commendation to the bodhisatvas and extensively filling all buddha-fields. He saw many clouds of manifestations of all the strata of gods belonging to the continuum of Brahma strongly issue from each and every hair from all his hair-pores, supplicating the manifest-buddha tathāgatas to turn the wheel of dharma. He saw many clouds of bodies of the Indra gods belonging to all the desire-realms issue forth from each and every hair from all his hair-pores, truly holding many dharma-wheels of all the tathāgatas. He saw clouds of buddha-fields similar to all the buddha-fields belonging to the three times **699** numerous as the extremely subtle atoms of all buddha-fields issue forth from each and every hair from all his hair-pores in each and every single moment of mind, which extensively filled all dharmadhātus infinite as the limits of space, turning into homes, shelters, and supports for sentient beings without home, shelter, or support. He saw clouds of completely pure buddha-fields, entirely filled with all the risen buddhas and retinue-maṇḍalas of bodhisatvas, numerous as the extremely subtle atoms of all buddha-fields strongly issue forth from each and every hair from all his hair-pores in every single moment of mind, which extensively filled all dharmadhātus infinite as the limits of space then produced entirely pure, tremendous intentions of sentient beings. He saw many clouds of completely purified totally afflicted buddha-fields numerous as the extremely subtle atoms of all buddha-fields strongly issue forth from each and every hair from all his hair-pores in every single moment of mind which, having extensively filled all the dharmadhātus infinite as the limits of the expanse of space, were accomplishing the complete purity of each totally afflicted sentient being. He saw many clouds of completely purified totally afflicted buddha-fields numerous as the extremely subtle atoms of all buddha-fields strongly issue forth from all his hairs from each hair-pore in every single moment of mind, extensively fill all dharmadhātus infinite as the limits of the expanse of space, accomplishing complete purity for the afflicted sentient beings as one. He saw clouds of bodies of all sentient beings numerous as the extremely subtle atoms of all buddha-fields strongly issue forth from each and every hair from all his hair-pores, **700** which extensively filled all sentient beings' makeups infinite as the expanse of space then were following after the conduct of all sentient beings and were thoroughly ripening all sentient beings into unsurpassed, truly complete enlightenment. He saw clouds of bodies of bodhisatvas numerous as the extremely subtle atoms of all world realms strongly issue forth from each and every hair from all his e hair-pores in every moment of mind, which extensively filled all dharmadhātus infinite as the expanse of space and then, in order to increase the roots of virtue of all sentient beings, were expressing many names of all buddhas. He saw clouds of bodies of bodhisatvas numerous as the extremely subtle atoms of all buddha-fields strongly issue forth from each and every hair from all his hair-pores, which extensively filled all dharmadhātus infinite as the expanse of space and then in all the infinite buddha fields' regions produced the accomplishment of all roots of virtue, from the initial generation of arousal of the mind to its full uptake, of all bodhisatvas. He saw clouds of bodhisatvas numerous as the extremely subtle atoms of all buddha-fields strongly issue forth from each and every hair from all his hair-pores who then in all the buddha-fields in order to produce the completely purity of bodhisatva Samantabhadra's conduct audibly expressed all the ocean-like prayers of the bodhisatva. He saw, for the sake of the thoughts of all sentient beings being fulfilled, a rain of clouds of bodhisatva Samantabhadra's conduct **701** that was increasing the force of their joy by truly causing them truly to arise in all-knowingness, numerous as the extremely subtle atoms of all buddha-fields, strongly issue forth from each and every hair from all his hair-pores, then strongly pour down. He saw clouds of beings who were becoming manifest complete buddhas showing becoming a manifest complete buddha in all the buddha-fields who were developing great clouds of the dharma causing arising in all-knowingness numerous as the extremely subtle atoms of all buddha-fields strongly issue forth.

Then the merchant's son Sudhana, due to having seen that kind of object of the miraculous display of the bodhisatva Samantabhadra, delightedly rejoiced, and, being gratified and pleased, was content and happy in mind. Then, as he paid even more attention to bodhisatva Samantabhadra's body, in each of the bodhisatva Samantabhadra's limbs, each section of his limbs, each of part of his body, each section of each part of his body, each area of his limbs, each section of each area of his limbs, each body, each section of body, each hair-pore, each section of each hair-pore, he saw in the manner of a reflection this great third-order thousand-fold world system together with its air aggregate, water aggregate, earth aggregate, fire aggregate, oceans, continents, rivers, precious mountains, Mount Sumeru, surrounds[12], villages and cities, lands and places and realms and king's places, forests, houses, **702** groups of beings, sentient being hell-worlds, animal birth-places, Lord of Death worlds, asura worlds, nāga worlds, garuḍa worlds, human worlds, god worlds, Brahmā worlds, desire-realm places, form-realm places, formless realm places, bases, supports, shapes, clouds, lightning, stars, solar days, half-months, full-months, seasons, years, intermediate aeons, aeons, and he saw all this as in the manner of a reflected image. Exactly as he saw this one so he also saw all of the world realms of the eastern directions. And exactly as he saw the ones in the eastern direction, so he also saw in the manner of a reflection all the world realms of all directions—the southern direction, the western direction, the northern direction, the north-eastern intermediate direction, the south-eastern intermediate direction, the south-western intermediate direction, the north-western intermediate direction, and the below and above directions—together with their risen buddhas and together with their retinue-maṇḍalas of bodhisatvas. He saw all, however many they are, one after another, the world systems to the earliest limit in the past before this Endurance World[13] from each of the marks of a great man of the bodhisatva Samantabhadra, together with **703** the risen buddhas, together with all retinue-mandalas of bodhisatvas, sentient beings, houses, solar days, and aeons. He also saw in the same way all the infinite buddha-fields till the latest limit in the future. Just as he saw one after another the world realms to the earliest and latest limits of the

---

[12] The surrounds of Mt. Meru are the seven rings of oceans containing the continents, the seven rings of iron mountains, and so on.

[13] For Endurance World, see the glossary.

past and future of this world realm, so he also saw all one after another of the world realms to the earliest and latest limits of the past and future of all the world realms of the ten directions for each body of Samantabhadra and each of his marks of a great man and from each hair pore down to each smallest section with none of the details of one another mixed up.

Moreover, how bodhisatva Samantabhadra was seen sitting on a precious lion-throne having the heart of a great lotus in the direct view of the bhagavan tathāgata Vairochana and fully showing this kind of play, he likewise also was seen in the eastern direction, sitting in the world realm Padmaśhrī of the tathāgata Bhadraśhrī, fully showing this same play. Just as in the east, likewise the bodhisatva Samantabhadra was also seen sitting on a precious lion-throne having the heart of a great lotus at the feet of all the tathāgatas of all world realms in all cardinal and intermediate directions, and fully showing this same play. **704** How he was seen sitting on a lion-throne having the heart of a great lotus at the feet of all tathāgatas of all the world realms of the ten directions and fully showing this same play, likewise, the bodhisatva Samantabhadra was seen in the extremely subtle atoms of all the buddha-fields of all ten directions, in the dharmadhātu-like vastnesses of the retinue-maṇḍalas of the buddhas of each of the extremely subtle atoms, sitting on a precious lion throne having the heart of a great lotus at the feet of all tathāgatas and fully showing this same play.

Each of those bodies moreover was seen to have strongly shown all the references that have arisen in the three times as references whose form was in the manner of a reflected image. They were seen to have strongly shown the references of all fields, all sentient beings, and all risen buddhas and all retinue-mandalas of bodhisatvas in the manner of a reflected image. He heard the sounds of all sentient beings, the voices of all buddhas, all special miracles of entirely teaching the dharma-wheels and oral instructions of all tathāgatas, all the bodhisatvas' authentic gatherings[14], and the plays of all buddhas. Having seen and heard in that way those sorts of play of the bodhisatva Samantabhadra, he gained ten types of living in the pāramitā of wisdom. What were the ten? They were as follows. **705** He gained the living in the pāramitā of wisdom in which he could extensively fill all buddha-fields with his body in one moment of mind. He gained the living in the pāramitā of wisdom in which there was no difference in going before the feet of all the tathāgatas. He gained the living in the pāramitā of wisdom in which he would make offerings to and honour all the tathāgatas. He gained the living in the pāramitā of wisdom in which he could utterly take up the entire petitioning of all and moreover each one of all the tathāgatas. He gained the living in the pāramitā of wisdom in which he could definitely comprehend the dharma-wheel of all tathāgatas. He gained the living in the pāramitā of wisdom in which he could perform a buddha's inconceivable transformations. He gained the living in the pāramitā of wisdom in which, having had inexhaustible individual authentic knowledge blessed to the aeon of the latest limit of the future, he could teach to the extreme one word of dharma. He gained the living in the pāramitā of wisdom in which he could utterly know in direct perception all dharma oceans. He gained the living in the pāramitā of wisdom of all the oceans of modes of dharmadhatu. He gained the living in the pāramitā of wisdom in which he could entirely accomplish the ideas of all sentient beings. **706** He gained the living in the pāramitā of wisdom in which he could, in one instant, utterly know in direct perception the conduct of bodhisatva Samantabhadra.

Then the bodhisatva Samantabhadra extended his right hand and placed it on the crown of the merchant's son Sudhana who now possessed those ways of living in the perfection of wisdom. Immediately the bodhisatva Samantabhadra had like that placed his hand on the merchant's son Sudhana's crown, he indeed entered into doors

---

[14] The gatherings are the four ways of gathering disciples explained in the Prajñāpāramitā sutras.

of samādhi numbering the extremely subtle atoms in all buddha-fields, and moreover, he also, through each of those samādhis, entered world realms numbering the extremely subtle atoms of the buddha-fields that had previously been unseen. His all-knowingness accumulation also became an accumulation in the amount of the extremely subtle atoms of all buddha-fields. His all-knowingness dharma accumulation rose also to the amount of the extremely subtle atoms of all buddha-fields. The great utterly staying in all-knowingness became elevated also by the amount of extremely subtle atoms of all buddha-fields. Prayer oceans became entered also in the amount of the extremely subtle atoms of all buddha-fields. The path on which one arises in all-knowingness rose also by the amount of extremely subtle atoms of all buddha-fields. The bodhisatva conduct became utterly entered also in the amount of the extremely subtle atoms of all buddha-fields. The intensity of the force for all-knowingness was increased also by the number of extremely subtle atoms of all buddha-fields. The appearances of the wisdom of all buddhas became utterly illuminated also by the number of extremely subtle atoms of all buddha-fields. **707**

Just as here in this Endurance World Samantabhadra sitting in direct view of the bhagavan tathāgata Vairochana extended his right hand and placed it on the crown of the merchant's son Sudhana, so the bodhisatva Samantabhadra sitting at the feet of the tathāgata of every world realm also extended his right hand and placed it on the crown of merchant's son Sudhana. Likewise, the bodhisatva Samantabhadra sitting at the feet of every tathāgata of the world realms contained within the extremely subtle atoms of the world realms of every one of all the cardinal and intermediate directions also extended his right hand and placed it on the crown of the merchant's son Sudhana. In the same way as the merchant's son Sudhana entered many dharma-gates on being touched by the hand of the bodhisatva Samantabhadra sitting at the feet of the bhagavan Vairochana, so the merchant's son Sudhanas who were contacted by the many clouds of hands reaching across from all the bodies of Samantabhadra also entered many dharma-doors in various ways.

Then, the bodhisatva mahāsatva Samantabhadra said this to the merchant's son Sudhana:

"Son of the family, did you just now see the transformations I made?"

He said:

"Noble one! What I saw was as much as I saw of an inconceivable complete emancipation; if a tathāgata were to know it **708** that would be the amount to be known."

He said:

"Son of the family, I strongly desired the mind of all-knowingness and worked at it for aeons numbering the extremely subtle atoms of the inexpressible buddha-fields, and in each of those great aeons, moreover, I was thoroughly purifying enlightenment mind[15] and I respectfully apprenticed myself to tathāgatas numerous as the extremely subtle atoms of those inexpressibly inexpressible buddha-fields. In each of those great aeons moreover, I was entirely collecting the merit of all-knowingness, was connecting with every type of great offering and giving, was becoming highly renowned in all worlds, and made the offering too of provisions for all sentient beings. In each of those great aeons, I was strongly aspiring for the dharma of all-knowingness and performed giving, great giving, and extremely great giving as much as the extremely subtle atoms of the inexpressibly inexpressible buddha-fields. In each of those great aeons, moreover, by placing no value on body and life but setting the buddha-dharma as that to be cherished, I gave up an inexpressibly inexpressible many bodies. I also gave up great kingdoms. I also gave up my cities, villages, lands, countries, realms, and royal seats. I also gave up retinues whose beauty and delight were not easy to let go of. I also gave up my sons, daughters, and wives. I also gave up my bodies and flesh. I also gave the blood from my bodies to those who requested it. I also gave my bones and marrow. **709** I also gave

---

[15] For enlightenment mind, see the glossary.

up my legs and arms. I also gave up my limbs and their parts. I also gave up my nose and ears. I also gave up my eyes. I also gave up my tongue-faculty from my own mouths. In each of those aeons, moreover, I had been strongly aspiring for a head[16] of all-knowingness that would be above and superior to the whole world and gave away my own head in an amount numbering the extremely subtle atoms of the inexpressibly inexpressible buddha-fields. Just as in each great aeon, likewise in each great aeon ocean, and in each of the aeon oceans derived from the numbering of extremely subtle atoms of inexpressibly inexpressible buddha-fields, I had moreover become an excellent faculty of and rendered service to tathāgatas numerous as the extremely subtle atoms of the inexpressibly inexpressible buddha-fields. I honoured them. I bowed to them. I offered clothing, food, bedding, medicine for sickness, and utensils. I went forth into the teaching of those tathāgatas and also fully entered all of the oral instructions of buddhas. I took ownership of their teachings, too.

"Son of the family! Throughout the aeon-oceans of that number moreover, I do not remember even a few times having aroused a mind not in harmony with the mind to be aroused for the tathāgata's teaching. Throughout the aeon-oceans of that number, I do not remember even a few times having aroused an angry mind, or a self-grasping mind, or a mind protective of and owning a self, **710** or a mind making a division between self and other, or a mind to leave the path of enlightenment, or a mind wearied by remaining in samsara, or a disheartened mind, or a mind of stupefied by obscuration. To the contrary, in order to accumulate the accumulation of all-knowingness, I always aroused the enlightenment mind, wisdom which cannot be affected by other and which possesses a core which is difficult to cross.

---

[16] This is a metaphor for "peak" but is used to tie it to the giving up of physical heads.

"Son of the family, it is thus. If I were to show you the perfections of my past yogas—the yoga of having entirely purified a buddha-field and thereby utterly gained the mind of great compassion, the yogas of having entirely protected sentient beings, working to thoroughly ripen them, and having thoroughly trained them, the yogas of offering to and respectfully apprenticing to the buddhas, the yogas of being respectful to the guru for the sake of seeking out the holy dharma, the yogas of having given up my body for the sake of owning the holy dharma, and the yogas of having given up my own life for the sake of guarding the holy dharma—it would take all of the aeon-oceans to do so.

"Son of the family! I, with even just a few words or letters from that number of dharma-oceans strived to protect all sentient beings, strived to know for certain my own mindstream, strived to actually hear dharma taught by others, strived to express all appearances of worldly wisdom, strived to utterly express all beyond-the-world wisdom, **711** strived to generate samsaric happiness for all sentient beings, and strived to truly commend the good qualities of all tathāgatas. By that, I have given up the sovereignty of a wheel-wielding king because of which no purchasing has been done, that is, by having given up on all material goods there has been nothing left unpurchased. Like that if I were to show you all the perfections of my own past yogas, it would take aeon-oceans numerous as the extremely subtle atoms of the inexpressibly inexpressible buddha-fields.

"Son of the family! In that way, I, by the strength of accumulations of that sort, the strength of accumulated causal roots of virtue, the strength of vast intent, the strength of being assiduous at good qualities, the strength of mastering all dharmas as they truly are, the strength of the eye of prajñā, the strength of tathāgata blessing, the strength of great prayers, the strength of great compassion, the strength of the extra-perceptions that come with having been thoroughly processed, the strength of being taken on by spiritual friends, have gained a entirely pure body of dharma that is not different in the three times. This unsurpassed body of form which is elevated over all worlds, references the types of thoughts just exactly as they are of all migrators, conforms with all of them, alights in all buddha-fields, utterly stays in all of them, shows all transformations in all aspects, has also been entirely purified into one that delights the minds of all migrators. **712**

"Son of the family! Behold this body I have gained which is perfect, which was accomplished during infinite aeon-oceans, which is difficult to come by and difficult to see in many hundreds of thousands of quadrillions of aeons!

"Son of the family! If I am not even heard of by sentient beings who have not created roots of virtue, then why mention their seeing me?!

"Son of the family! There are sentient beings who merely by hearing my name become irreversible from unsurpassed, truly complete enlightenment. There are also those who by merely seeing, merely escorting, merely touching, merely following me, merely seeing me in a dream, or merely hearing my name in a dream become irreversible from unsurpassed, truly complete enlightenment. Some sentient beings will become thoroughly ripened if they remember me for a day. Some will become thoroughly ripened if they recall me for seven days, some for half a month, some for one month, some for one year, some for one hundred years, some for one aeon, some for one hundred aeons, some for aeons as numerous as the extremely subtle atoms of the inexpressibly inexpressible buddha-fields. Some will become thoroughly ripened if they recall me for a lifetime. Some will become thoroughly ripened because of a string of lives numerous as the extremely subtle atoms of the inexpressibly inexpressible buddha-fields. Some sentient beings will become thoroughly ripened by seeing my light. **713** Some will become thoroughly ripened by seeing my emitted light rays, some by movement of the field, some by being shown my form-body, and some by having been pleased. Son of the family! By types of method like that numerous as the extremely subtle atoms of a buddha-field sentient beings will become irreversible from unsurpassed, truly complete enlightenment.

"Son of the family! Sentient beings who hear of my entirely pure buddha-field will be born in an entirely pure buddha-field. Ones who see my entirely pure body will be born in a body like mine. Therefore, son of the family, behold my complete purity body!"

Then, the merchant's son Sudhana put his attention onto the body of bodhisatva Samantabhadra and saw each hair-pore entirely filled with buddhas of inexpressibly inexpressible buddha-field oceans. In each of those field-oceans, moreover, he saw many tathāgatas present, totally surrounded by their retinue-oceans of bodhisatvas. All of those field oceans, moreover, he saw having various grounds, various shapes, various ornaments, various surrounds, various clouds, various skies covering them, various buddhas arising, and voices of various dharma-wheels. Exactly as with each hair-pore, likewise in all hair-pores without exception and all the excellent marks and all the illustrative signs and all limbs and their parts, he saw from each and every field ocean clouds of manifested buddha-bodies numerous as the extremely subtle atoms of all buddha-fields extensively fill all the world realms in the ten directions **714** then do the deed of thoroughly ripening sentient beings into unsurpassed, truly complete enlightenment.

Then, the merchant's son Sudhana, having been taught by the oral instructions and teachings of the bodhisatva Samantabhadra, entered into all the world realms included within the body of bodhisatva Samantabhadra, where he became active in thoroughly ripening sentient beings.

In that way, the merchant's son Sudhana went before spiritual friends numbering the extremely subtle atoms of the buddha-fields where, by seeing and respectfully apprenticing to them, he accumulated wisdom appearances and roots of virtue. However, they did not come close to being even one hundredth part of the roots of virtue he accumulated by seeing the bodhisatva Samantabhadra. They were not even a thousandth part, nor even a hundred-thousandth part, nor even a one-hundred billionth part of them; they could not come up to a fraction of a number or count or example or cause of them.

There were, from the first time he had aroused the mind and fully taken it up until the time he saw the bodhisatva Samantabhadra, the entrances he had made into however many, one after another, buddha field oceans. Going from those up to the number of extremely subtle atoms in the inexpressibly inexpressible buddha-fields, he entered in one instant of mind into many one after another buddha-field oceans in each of the hair pores of the bodhisatva Samantabhadra. And, moreover, exactly as in each hair-pore, likewise in all hair-pores without exception, he trod in each moment of mind through world realms numbering the extremely subtle atoms of inexpressibly inexpressible world realms, blessing them to the aeon of the latest limit of the future, entering the world realms by extensively filling them, **715** but never finished passing one after another through field-oceans; he did not arrive at a finish of the mass of field-oceans, the specifics of field-oceans, the whole of field-oceans, the production of field-oceans, the perishing of field-oceans, the classifying of field-oceans, the passing one after another through buddhas-risen oceans, the bodies of buddhas-risen oceans, the specifics of buddhas-risen oceans, the whole of buddhas-risen oceans, the arising of buddhas-risen oceans, the perishing of buddhas-risen oceans, the classifying of buddhas-risen oceans, the maṇḍala-oceans of bodhisatva retinues, the passing one after another through maṇḍala-oceans of bodhisatva retinues, the bodies of maṇḍala-oceans of bodhisatva retinues, the specifics of maṇḍala-oceans of bodhisatva-retinues, the whole of maṇḍala-oceans of bodhisatva retinues, the arising of maṇḍala-oceans of bodhisatva retinues, the destruction of maṇḍala-oceans of bodhisatva retinues, entering into the makeups of sentient beings, entering moment by moment into knowing the faculties of sentient beings, mastering of knowledge of the faculties of sentient beings, the thorough ripening and taming of sentient beings, completely abiding in profound bodhisatva's transformation, or wholly treading the bodhisatva levels.

He lived in some fields for aeons. He acted in some fields for aeons as many as inexpressibly inexpressible buddha fields and without moving from them. **716** In each moment of mind, moreover, he was entering field oceans without edge or centre and also, for the sentient beings there, was thoroughly ripening them into unsurpassed, truly complete enlightenment. He came in that way up to the limit of seeing sameness with the conduct and prayer oceans of bodhisatva Samantabhadra. He gained, following him, sameness with the tathāgatas, sameness with extensively filling all fields with bodies, sameness with extensively filling conduct to completion, sameness with extensively filling by showing the transformation of becoming a manifest complete buddha, sameness with turning the dharma wheel, sameness with the complete purity of individual authentic knowing, sameness with expressing the voice, sameness with the yoga of all the ocean-like aspects of voice, sameness in strengths and fearlessness, sameness with living as a buddha, sameness with great loving kindness and great compassion, and sameness in the inconceivable transformations belonging to a bodhisatva's complete emancipations.

Then, the bodhisatva mahāsatva Samantabhadra who had trod those aeons and infinite aeons and world realms one after another numbering the extremely subtle atoms of the inexpressible buddha-fields made, in order to express clearly what he had shown, this prayer in melodious verse:

However many they are, all the lions of men gone
In the three times in the worlds of the ten directions,
I prostrate to all of them without exception,
With admiring body, speech, and mind.

Through the forces of excellent conduct prayer
All conquerors are seen in direct perception by mind;
Through utterly bowing with bodies many as the field atoms,
I utterly prostrate to all the conquerors.

On a single atom buddhas many as atoms
Are seated at the centre of buddha sons;
I imagine in that way that all the dharmadhātus
Without exception are filled with conquerors.

Those oceans of unending commendation
Have using all sounds of the ocean of aspects of the voice
The good qualities of all the conquerors utterly expressed
And I praise all of the ones gone to bliss.

I will make offerings to those conquerors
With the finest flowers, finest garlands,
Small cymbals, ointments, supreme parasols,
Supreme oil lamps, and finest incense.

I will make offerings to those conquerors
With the finest clothes, supreme scents,
And mixed powders equal to Mt. Meru,
And all with the best of excellent displays.

The offerings which are unsurpassed, vaster,
Those are also imagined for all the conquerors.
Through the forces of faith in excellent conduct
I will prostrate and offer to all the conquerors.

Under the influence of desire, anger, and delusion
And through body, speech, and likewise mind,
The evils I have done whichever they might be,
I lay all of them aside, each one individually.

I rejoice in all merits whoever has them,
Those of all the conquerors of the ten directions and
The buddha sons, of the pratyekabuddhas, of those
In training and not in training, and of all migrators.

Ones who are lamps of the worlds of the ten directions
Have become buddhas at the enlightenment stage and gained the
    undefiled state;
I urge all of those guardians
To turn the unsurpassed wheel.

I also will supplicate with palms joined together those
Who have asserted they will show passage into nirvana
To stay for aeons as many as the field atoms
In order to bring benefit and ease to all migrators.

I dedicate every trifle of virtue that
I have accumulated in prostrating, offering,
Laying aside, rejoicing, urging, and supplicating
For the purpose of enlightenment.

May I offer to the past buddhas and the ones
Who are seated in the worlds of the ten directions.
Those whoever have not descended, most quickly completing
    your intentions
Descend to buddhahood at the enlightenment stage!

May the fields which exist in the ten directions,
However many they are, be vast and wholly pure.
May they be utterly filled with conquerors gone
Before the leading bodhi tree and with buddha sons.

May the sentient beings of the ten directions,
However many, always be free of sickness and have ease.
May all migrators' objectives of dharma be with
Harmony and their hopes also be accomplished.

While I perform the conducts of enlightenment
May I remember my births in all migrations.
At death transfers and births in all successive lives
May I always become ordained.

May I train following all the conquerors,
Working to wholly complete the excellent conduct
And doing the stainless, totally pure discipline conduct
In a way that is always uncorrupted and faultless.

I will teach dharma in all languages—
In gods, nāgas, and yakṣhas' languages,
In khumbandha and mens' languages and
In all migrators' languages many as there are.

Gentled, I'll be most diligent at the pāramitās;
I will never forget enlightenment mind.
May the evils become obscurations
Without exception be totally cleansed.

May I be free of karma, affliction, and māra's works,
And though as migrators of the world, have conduct
Which is like the way a lotus is unaffected by water,
And like the sun and moon are unhindered in the sky.

For as much as the area of a field and directions
I'll utterly pacify the suffering of the bad migrations
Then set all migrators in the best of happinesses;
I will perform conduct that benefits all migrators.

I will work at completing enlightenment conduct,
Enter in harmony with sentient beings' conduct,
And utterly teach the excellent conducts;
May I do this throughout all future aeons.

May I always be accompanied by those
Whose conduct matches my own!
Moreover, through body, speech, and mind
I will perform the same conducts and prayer.

Companions who wish to benefit me,
The ones who utterly teach excellent conduct—
May I always be with them!
I will never displease them!

I will always view the conquerors in direct perception,
The guardians, buddhas surrounded by their sons.
I will also make vast offerings to them
In all future aeons without wearying.

Holding the holy dharma of the conquerors
And fully illuminating enlightenment conduct,
I will completely purify the excellent conduct
And moreover will do that in all future aeons.

May I in re-entering all becomings
Acquire unending merits and wisdoms.
May I become an unending store of method, prajñā,
Samādhis, complete emancipations, and all good qualities.

On one atom are fields as many as the atoms
And in those fields inconceivable buddhas
Seated at the centre of their buddha sons;
Doing enlightenment conduct, I will view them.

Like that so too in all directions without exception
On the breadth of merely a hair there's an ocean of buddhas
Many as their measure in the three times and an ocean of fields
And for an ocean of aeons doing the conduct, I'll utterly enter
   them.

Through the ocean of branches of sound in one speech,
The complete purity of the branches of voice of all conquerors,
Coming as voices exactly in accord with all migrators' thoughts,
The buddha speech, is what I will perpetually enter.

All the conquerors gone in the three times'
Utter turning of the modes of the wheel
And also their unending voices of speech
I too will, by the force of rational mind, utterly enter.

The entering into all future aeons is something
That I too will do but in merely an instant.
Whatever the extent of aeons in the three times
I will act to have entered them in a fraction of an instant.

I will view in a single instant
The lions of men gone in the three times.
I will perpetually enter their domains by
The force of the illusory complete emancipation.

Whatever the field arrangements of the three times,
I will make them manifest on a single atom.
Like that in all the directions without exception,
I will enter the ornamentation of conquerors' fields.

Whichever lamps of the world have not descended
Will become buddhas at the stage, turn the wheel,
And show nirvana, the final, utter peace.
I will go before all those guardians.

Forces of miracles which have all speed,
Forces of vehicle which is in all ways a door,
Forces of conduct whose quality is always good,
Force of loving kindnesses which are all pervasive,

Forces of merit which is all virtuous,
Forces of wisdom become without defilement,
Forces of prajñā, method, and samādhi—by them
I'll be truly accomplishing the forces of enlightenment.

Wholly purifying the forces of karma,
Totally destroying the forces of affliction, and
Utterly rendering powerless the forces of māra,
The forces of excellent conduct will be completed.

I will be completely purifying an ocean of fields,
Completely liberating the ocean of sentient beings,
Utterly seeing an ocean of dharmas,
Utterly realizing an ocean of wisdom,

Completely purifying an ocean of conduct,
Wholly completing an ocean of prayers,
Utterly offering to an ocean of buddhas,
And doing so tirelessly for an ocean of aeons.

The conquerors gone in the three times had their
Particular prayers of enlightenment conduct;
Becoming an enlightened buddha by excellent conduct,
I will complete all their prayers without exception.

The chief of the sons of all the conquerors is
The one whose name is "Samantabhadra"—
I utterly dedicate all these virtues here in order
To conduct myself with expertise equalling his.

The way he is expert at excellent dedications for
Completely pure body, speech, and mind, and
Completely pure conduct, and wholly pure fields,
May I too be equal to him in the same way.

For thoroughly virtuous excellent conduct
I will act as in the prayer of Mañjuśhrī.
Without wearying in all future aeons
I will complete their works without exception.

May my conducts not become measurable.
May my good qualities also be immeasurable.
Due to remaining in conduct without measure
I will know all of their transformations.

As far as it would be to the final end of space
And to the end of every sentient being likewise,
And as much as to the end of karma and affliction,
It will also be that much to the end of my prayer.

Compared to one who adorns the infinite fields wherever in the
    ten directions
With jewels and offers that to the conquerors,
And offers the most enjoyable things of gods and men
For aeons as many as the atoms of the fields,

The one who hears this king of dedications
Then is utterly inspired towards and even just one time
Gives rise to faith in supreme enlightenment
Is the one who has the better superior merits.

Someone who has made this excellent conduct prayer
Will have abandoned all bad migrations,
He will have abandoned bad companions,
And he will also see Amitābha soon.

They acquire the best, are sustained in goodness,
And even in this human life can turn out well.
Moreover, whatever Samantabhadra is like,
Before long they will become like that too.

The evil deeds of the five immediates done by
Someone under the control of not knowing will,
If he recites this excellent conduct prayer,
Be quickly and without exception wholly cleansed.

He will possess wisdom, form,
Marks, family, and colour.
Many māras and Tīrthikas will be unable to affect him;
In all three worlds even offerings will be made to him.

He'll quickly go to the foot of the leading bodhi tree
And, having done so, in order to benefit sentient beings,
Will sit there, become an enlightened buddha, utterly turn the
    wheel,
And tame all the māras together with their regiments.

For whoever holds, reads or teaches
This prayer of excellent conduct
Their full-ripenings will be known by buddha.
Do not be sceptical of supreme enlightenment!

Mañjushrī knows how it is and is heroic
And Samantabhadra is like that too;
Following them in every way, I train and
Will utterly dedicate all of these virtues.

Using the dedication which all the conquerors
Gone in the three times commend as supreme,
I utterly dedicate all these roots of virtue of mine
For the purpose of excellent conduct.

When the time has come for me to die,
May all obscurations clear away;
Seeing Amitābha in direct perception,
I will utterly go to the field of Sukhāvatī.

Having gone there, may all these prayers
Without exception become manifest.
Having completely fulfilled them without exception,
I will benefit sentient beings as long as the world.

In that good and pleasing maṇḍala of the conqueror
May I be born from an exceptionally beautiful fine lotus.
Seeing conqueror Amitābha directly,
May I also obtain the prophecy there.

Having completely obtained the prophecy there,
I will with many thousands of millions of emanations
By force of rational mind, throughout the ten directions
Do many things to benefit sentient beings.

May the trifle of virtue accumulated by the one
Who has recited this excellent conduct prayer
Cause the virtues of migrators' prayers
To be obtained by them all in an instant.

May whatever infinite superior merit has been gained
In wholly dedicating this excellent conduct prayer
Cause migrators drowning in the river of unsatisfactoriness
To utterly gain the place of Amitābha.

From the great enumeration of dharmas called *Gaṇḍavyūha*, a part of the bodhisatva section of the extremely large sutra known as the *Avataṃsaka*, one part of Subhuti's respectful conduct when attending to spiritual friends is, in total, complete.

The above was translated into Tibetan language from Sanskrit then corrected and finalized by the Indian preceptors Jinamitra and Surendrabodhi, the chief editor Lotsāwa Bande Yeshe De, and others.

*Samantabhadra's Prayer
Extracted and Arranged for use
by Tibetans*

Noble One, A King of Prayers of Excellent Conduct

In Indian language: āryabhadracaryāpraṇidhānarājā.
In Tibetan language: 'phags pa bzang po spyod pa'i smon lam gyi rgyal po.

I prostrate to noble Mañjuśrī who has become youthful.

[The prayer extracted from its original place in the Gaṇḍavyūha Sutra is inserted here.]

The chief of these supreme prayers in this king of prayers
Brings benefit to all the infinite migrators;
May this scripture adorned with Samantabhadra be accomplished
And all the places of bad migrations be emptied.

Noble One, A King of Prayers of Excellent Conduct is complete.

Translated, corrected, and finalized by the Indian preceptors Jinamitra and Surendrabodhi, the chief editor Lotsāwa Bande Yeshe De, and others.

*Samantabhadra's Prayer
Extracted and Arranged for use
by non-Tibetans*

Samantabhadra's Prayer
A King of Prayers of Excellent Conduct

The following is extracted from the fifty-third chapter of the Gaṇḍavyūha Sutra in which Subhuti goes before the bodhisatva Samantabhadra to gain further insight into the meaning of the Great Vehicle.

Then, the bodhisatva mahāsatva Samantabhadra who had trod those aeons and infinite aeons and world realms one after another numbering the extremely subtle atoms of the inexpressible buddha-fields made, in order to express clearly what he had shown, this prayer in melodious verse:

[The prayer is presented in full here.]

From the great enumeration of dharmas called *Gaṇḍavyūha*, a part of the bodhisatva section of the extremely large sutra known as the *Avataṃsaka*, one part of Subhuti's respectful conduct when attending to spiritual friends is, in total, complete.

The above was translated into Tibetan language from Sanskrit then corrected and finalized by the Indian preceptors Jinamitra and Surendrabodhi, the chief editor Lotsāwa Bande Yeshe De, and others.

This arrangement for the practice of Samantabhadra's Prayer for Westerners was made by the Australian translator Tony Duff at the buddhas' place of Swayambunath, Nepal, in the spring of 2013 after consulting many Indian and Tibetan commentaries to the prayer. To remove the errors which have crept into Tibetan arrangements of the prayer, the prayer itself was translated from the sutra as found in the Derge edition of the Kangyur.

A Commentary to Samantabhadra's Prayer
By
Tenpa'i Wangchuk Rinpoche

Plate 2. Ontrul Tenpa'i Wangchuk at the Sanctuary of
Elaboration-Free Alpha Purity,
Golok, Tibet, 2007. Picture by the author.

"The Enlightenment Highway"

A Commentary to the Prayer of Excellent Conduct
Or Notes of This and That Remembered,
Written as Practical Instructions for
Men and Women Householders
Encouraging them to Virtue

by Tenpa'i Wangchuk

Contents

The Virtue of the Beginning, the Prefatory Topics

1. The Meaning of the Title 49
2. The Translator's Prostration 53

The Virtue of the Middle, the Actual Topics of the Text

1. The Cause for Doing the Prayer, the Seven Limbs of Accumulation 58
   1. The limb of prostration 58
      1. The synopsis 58
      2. The extended explanation 60
         1. Prostration through body 60
         2. Prostration through mind 62
         3. Prostration through speech 66
   2. The limb of making offerings 68
      1. Surpassable offering 68
      2. Unsurpassable offering 73
   3. The limb of laying aside evil 76
   4. The limb of rejoicing 80
   5. The limb of urging to turn the dharma wheel 82

      6. The limb of supplicating to remain, not passing
         into nirvana 84
      7. The limb of dedicating all roots of virtue to
         enlightenment 85
  2. An Extensive Explanation of the Divisions of the Actual
    Prayer 88
    1. The Main Part 88
      1. Prayer for pure thought 89
        1. Prayer for offering to the buddhas 89
        2. Prayer to wholly fulfil the intent 89
        3. Prayer to purify a buddha-field 90
        4. Prayer to benefit sentient beings 92
      2. Prayer for not forgetting enlightenment mind . 93
        1. Prayer for remembering the succession of
          lives 94
        2. Prayer for being ordained 96
        3. Prayer for pure discipline 98
        4. Prayer to be able to teach dharma in various
          languages 99
        5. Prayer for making effort at virtue 101
        6. Prayer not to forget enlightenment mind . 102
        7. Prayer to be free from adverse
          circumstances 104
      3. Prayer for conduct which is uncloaked or
        undefiled 105
      4. Prayer to set sentient beings in benefit and ease 108
      5. Prayer for wearing armour 109
      6. Prayer to have the company of companions of
        the same lot 111
      7. Prayer to attend to and please a virtuous
        spiritual friend 113
      8.
        1. Prayer for making the tathāgata's visible . 114
        2. Having seen their faces, a prayer to make
          offerings 114
      9. A prayer for wholly holding the holy dharma 115

10. Prayer for acquiring an unending store 116
11. Prayer for entering, having eight enterings . 118
   1. Entering viewing the fields and buddhas—
      two types 118
   2. Entering the buddha speech 120
   3. Entering into turning the dharma wheel . 121
   4. Prayer to enter aeons 122
   5. Entering into viewing the tathāgatas 123
   6. Prayer to enter their domain 124
   7. Prayer for entering into intention and
      production 124
   8. Prayer to enter going before the tathāgatas 126
12. Prayer for forces 127
13. Prayer for accomplishing the antidote 129
14. Prayer for enlightened activity 130
15. Prayer for training following 132
   1. Prayer to train following the buddhas ... 132
   2. Prayer to train following the two supreme
      bodhisatvas 133
      1. Prayer to train following
         Samantabhadra 133
      2. Prayer to train following Mañjughoṣha 134

The Virtue of the End,
the Concluding Topics of the Text

16. Concluding dedication 136
2. Showing the end of the prayer 137
3. Showing the advantages then concluding 138
   1. The prayer's advantages 138
      1. The synopsis 138
      2. Full explanation 140
      3. The meaning summed up through benefits 147
   2. Dedication of the prayer with benefits
      (dedication of having kept, written, and

recited while keeping the meaning in mind
this prayer) 148
1. Dedication in connection with the great
   bodhisatvas Mañjushrī and Samantabhadra
   148
2. Entering into conquerors' dedications or
   entering how the buddhas would pray .. 149
3. Dedication for the result of the prayer to be
   manifest 150
4. Dedication or prayer to actually obtain the
   prophecy from a buddha 151
5. Having obtained the prophecy, a prayer to
   accomplish benefit for sentient beings .. 152
6. Other dedications 153

The Virtue of the Beginning, The Prefatory Topics

1. The Meaning of the Title

In Indian language: āryabhadracharyāpraṇidhānarājā
In Tibetan language: 'phags pa bzang po spyod pa'i smon lam gyi rgyal po
[In English language: Noble One, A King of Prayers of Excellent Conduct]

Generally speaking, in India in the past there were three hundred and sixty different languages of which four were universally known, major languages: the well-constructed or Sanskrit language known as the language of the gods; the devolved, common form of it, known as Prakrit; the less strict forms of it also known as "corrupted languages", the Avabhraṃsha languages; and the language of the flesh-eating spirits, known as Piśhāci. It is well known that the common perception amongst disciples when the Buddha Bhagavat turned the three stages of the wheel of dharma was that, of those major languages, he spoke in the language of the gods, Sanskrit. Thus, the name of this text *in* that ***Indian language*** is "*āryabhadracharyāpraṇidhānarājā*". That is expressed *in the **Tibetan language*** with " *'phags pa bzang po spyod pa'i smon lam gyi rgyal po*" [and in English with "Noble One, A King of Prayers of Excellent Conduct"]. When the words of the languages are cross-referenced: "ārya" is 'phags pa [noble one]; "bhadra" is bzang po [excellent];

"charyā" is spyod pa [conduct]; "praṇidhāna" is smon lam [prayer]; and "rāja" is rgyal po [king].

It has been said that, generally speaking, this bodhisatva's prayer contains two types of prayer: prayers for enlightenment conduct and prayers for excellent conduct. Minyag Kunso when explaining *Maitreya's Prayer*[17] said to me:

> *The Excellent Conduct Prayer* is, like *Maitreya's Prayer*, a prayer of enlightenment and excellent conduct. The difference between the two is as follows. If we look at the composers of these prayers, in the case of Maitreya who took the approach of a being a guardian, the arousing of mind involved was like that of a king who aspires first to gain buddhahood himself then after that to set all sentient beings on the level of a buddha. That sort of arousing of mind is called "great aspiration" and is less courageous. A prayer made that way is an enlightenment conduct type of prayer. In the case of the bodhisatva Samantabhadra and also of Mañjuśhrī in his prayer, the arousing of mind was the type that aspires first to set every sentient being on the level of a buddha then after that to gain the rank of buddhahood for onself. That sort of arousing of mind has the approach of being a herder and is a great arousing of mind. A prayer made that way is referred to as "a prayer of excellent conduct".

Now, if we look at the words of the title, some commentaries say that it means "a prayer of the excellent conduct of those who are at the level of noble ones". However, the oral tradition of The Expert Glorious King's[18] commentary, which is the one we are following

---

[17] See *Maitreya's Sutras and Prayer with Commentary by Padma Karpo* by Tony Duff.

[18] This is a name which Dza Patrul Chokyi Wangpo gave to himself in
(continued ...)

here, explains that this excellent conduct prayer belongs to the Abhidharma section of the three baskets of the Great Vehicle whose literature is demarcated from that of the Lesser Vehicle by prepending the word "noble one" to the title, so the words of the title mean "literature of the noble vehicle, an excellent conduct prayer".[19]

Next, this text spoken by the Noble Samantabhadra to the youthful Sudhana belongs to the section of dharma concerned with training in the bodhisatva's conduct and that is outstanding or supreme compared to all other sections of dharma, so the prayer is called "a prayer of excellent conduct". And then, because the prayer fully shows the way to carry out the excellent conduct of the six pāramitās motivated by the excellent thought of enlightenment mind, it is a

---

[18](... continued) his writings. He was an *expert* in the Buddhist teachings and in Dzogchen literature gave himself the name *Glorious King* because of his realization of the Dzogchen teachings.

[19] The term "noble one" at the beginning of a title in Tibetan Buddhist literature usually demarcates literature of the Great Vehicle". However, it can be the title "noble one" used to indicate a person who has reached a noble level of spiritual attainment. This debate over the meaning of the title comes from Tibetan experts not bothering to read the Indian commentaries to the prayer. If they had, they would know that the Indian commentaries simply do not have "noble one" in the title and that the term "noble one" was added to the title when the Tibetans translated it from Sanskrit in order to show that it was literature from the Great Vehicle. Thus, the correct understanding of the Tibetan title is "Noble One, A King of Prayers of Excellent Conduct", but the true translation of the title is simply "A King of Prayers of Excellent Conduct" without the "noble one" later added by Tibetans. (Someone might see that the Sanskrit title shown on the previous page does begin with "ārya" meaning "noble one". However, that title is not the original Sanskrit title but has "ārya" added to it by the Tibetans for the reasons mentioned above.)

prayer that is more than supreme, and there is no other way to indicate that except to call it "a king of prayers".

Generally speaking, there have been many claims about how many individual prayers this prayer contains, such as "three hundred thousand great prayers" and "five hundred great prayers", and so on. However, it is taught that when the prayer is distilled down, it consists of sixteen major prayers that include everything within it. If those sixteen prayers that constitute the whole *Prayer of Excellent Conduct* are distilled down again, they are contained within the four-line verse in the concluding section of the prayer that starts "Mañjushrī the hero …"[20]

Moreover, it has been taught that the personal capacity needed to actually perform what is described in *Noble One, A Prayer for Excellent Conduct* in its entirety is found only in those who have attained the path of the noble ones by having attained the first bodhisatva level and up. *Entering the Middle Way* says, "It is a first-level person who fully performs Samantabhadra's prayer", which means that the personal capacity needed to actually make these prayers is found in those who have attained the first level, that is, the path of seeing. It has been taught that others who have not reached that level—the bodhisatvas on the paths of accumulation and connection, and the shrāvakas, pratyekas, and so on—do not have the personal capacity needed to actually make these prayers.

---

[20] This explanation of sixteen main topics of prayer within the body of the prayer and all of them being summed up in the prayer that begins "Mañjushrī the hero" is a tradition of explanation that started long ago in India. For example, the earliest available commentary, by Noble Nāgārjuna, explains it this way. The verse referred to has two distinctly different translations into Tibetan. The wording of the other translation is "Mañjushrī knows how it is and is heroic …"

2. The Translator's Prostration

I prostrate to noble Mañjushrī who has become youthful.

The translator's prostration is made either because of following the king's edict that such must be made or to identify the section of the Buddha's teachings to which the subject matter belongs. The dharma in this text belongs to the Abhidharma section and the prostration here primarily shows that what is to be expressed is the higher training of prajñā, so the prostration identifies the section. Then again, prior to and separate from the actual translation, a translator often makes a prostration to his own special deity, whichever it is, so this also includes the translator's prostration.

This is what it is saying: *I prostrate* with respectful three doors *to* Mañjushrī who, being above ordinary beings, or who, being above the two possibilities of becoming and peace, is *noble*. He has divorced himself from the coarseness of the afflictions so is *mañju* meaning soft. He has the glory of non-dual bliss-emptiness wisdom or has the glory of the six qualities of "goodness"[21], so is *shrī* or glorious[22]. He *has become a* son of all the conquerors who, divorced

---

[21] "Having the six qualities of goodness" is explained as one of the meanings of "bhagavat" and anyone who is a bhagavat is also glorious. A complete explanation of bhagavat, including the six goodnesses, can be found in *Unending Auspiciousness, the Sutra of the Recollection of the Noble Three Jewels* by Tony Duff.

[22] "Soft and glorious" is the literal translation of Mañjushrī's name, as has been explained here.

from the failings of birth, death, and aging, is a *youthful* Zur Phud Ngapa, with the fresh qualities of a sixteen year old[23].

Many commentaries to this excellent conduct prayer were composed in the Noble Land of India by noble Nāgārjuna and the masters Dignāga, Shākyamitra, Bhadravaha, and others. In Tibet too, commentaries were composed by the Jonang Jetsuns Tāranātha and Kunkhyen Tobbar Ozer, by Changkya Rolpa'i Dorje, and Minling's Lochen Dharmaśhrī[24], and others.

The commentaries of the Jonang Jetsuns Tāranātha and Kunkhyen Tobbar Ozer are moderately extensive. Changkya Rolpa'i Dorje's is fifty-five folios in length. Changkya's commentary provides us with the literal meaning as spoken. The commentaries of both noble Nāgārjuna and master Dignāga—the first a full explanation of the prayer and the second an abbreviated one—are very consistent and, given that those masters were great experts of the Noble Land, have to be regarded as the ones that truly maintain our tradition. Jetsun Tāranātha's commentary connects the prayer only with the high bodhisatva levels, so has many places where it does not agree with the other texts. Kunkhyen Tobbar Ozer's commentary follows Shākyamitra's commentary in a general way, though some say that it is not like Shakyamitra's commentary because it tries to connect the content of the prayer with the ten levels and ten pāramitās, making it hard for it to stay consistent with the explanations given in the great Indian texts of Buddhism, and for that reason I was told not to attempt to analyze and comment on it. Changkya's way of

---

[23] Zur Phud Ngapa is the name of a leader of the gandharvas, a race of non-human spirits like European fairies. The name means that he has long tresses of hair, which in Asian thought is a sign of youth and virility. In addition, because he is a fairy, mention of his name evokes a sense of a light-filled being of great radiance and youth. A sixteen year old is the epitome of youth because the internal factors of the body reach their peak at that age.

[24] "Lochen" is the Tibetan for "Great Translator".

connecting the prayer first with the four intentional conducts then with the ten bodhisatva levels in sequence from one to ten means that it is different in many places with the commentaries of those two Jonang masters. Despite all of that, given that our way as found in Dzogchen Patrul's flawless oral tradition is available in the bitwise commentary of Adzom Gyalsay, I have made it the primary source for this commentary[25].

I have been taught the following. In general, no matter which prayer you make, for the accomplishment of great prayers you must first set a foundation of completely pure discipline. In other words, prayers are a time for pure discipline or virtues. On top of that, in accordance with what all prayers say—"May this be accomplished according to my wishes"—the conditions for the accomplishment of prayers—gathering the accumulations and cleansing the obscurations—are important because without those conditions, whatever prayers you make might or might not be accomplished. Thus, if you have assembled both the cause—completely pure discipline—and the conditions—gathering the accumulations and cleansing the obscurations—no matter which prayer you make, it will definitely be accomplished.

For this particular prayer, a study of it begins with the story behind it. The prayer is recorded in the *Avataṃsaka Sutra* together with the story of how it came about. Previously, the bodhisatva youthful Sudhana attended one hundred and ten virtuous friends of whom the last was the bodhisatva called "Samantabhadra". When he met Samantabhadra, it is said that youthful Sudhana "was able to enter the ocean-like maṇḍala of Samantabhadra", and this is what that means. When youthful Sudhana first came face-to-face with the bodhisatva called Samantabhadra, that bodhisatva Samantabhadra

---

[25] It is "our way" because Dzogchen Patrul was one of the early mainstays of the Dzogchen Monastery tradition and Tenpa'i Wangchuk is a member of that tradition. Bitwise commentary is explained in the introduction, in the section about Tenpa'i Wangchuk's commentary.

was present before the bhagavat Vairochana, seated on the bed of a lotus on a lion throne of precious substances, surrounded by an ocean-like assembly of bodhisatvas. In front of that Vairochana, moreover, was a bodhisatva Samantabhadra surrounded by a retinue of an unfathomable number of bodhisatvas. Not only that, but within each of the hair pores of that bodhisatva Samantabhadra an ocean[26] of field realms and an ocean of buddhas with oceans of retinues of bodhisatvas surrounding them. In front of the one Vairochana buddha present there, the bodhisatva Samantabhadra sent out unfathomable displays of bodies so that in front of each buddha of all the buddhas of the ten directions were inconceivable bodhisatva Samantabhadras and inconceivable retinues of bodhisatvas, and in each of the hair pores of each of the Samantabhadras were inconceivable field realms, inconceivable Samantabhadras, inconceivable buddhas, and inconceivable retinue bodhisatvas. Likewise, in front of all the buddhas displayed such that on each single atom there were as many of them as the atoms of the world realms, there were inconceivable bodhisatva Samantabhadras with inconceivable retinue bodhisatvas, in each of whose hair pores were inconceivable field realms, inconceivable Samantabhadras, inconceivable buddhas, and inconceivable retinue bodhisatvas. That inconceivable deed pervaded everywhere that space pervades, everywhere that dharmadhātu pervades, and in accordance with that there were inconceivable Samantabhadras, inconceivable buddhas, and inconceivable retinue bodhisatvas. Like that within each of the hair pores of each of the Samantabhadras, were inconceivable field realms, inconceivable Samantabhadras, and inconceivable retinue bodhisatvas. That sort of thing is what youthful Sudhana met in direct perception. That is what was meant by saying: "Youthful Sudhana was able to enter the ocean-like field realms of Samantabhadra".

---

[26] "Ocean" is used in Sanskrit as a metaphor for something unending. Therefore, the prayer usually does not say "oceans of" but "an ocean of" meaning an unending amount of whatever is being discussed.

At that point, bodhisatva Samantabhadra extended his right hand like an elephant extending its trunk and, having placed it on top of youthful Sudhana's head, spoke the first words of this excellent conduct prayer "However many they are …"

The Virtue of the Middle, The Actual Topics of the Text

1. The Cause of Doing the Prayer, the Seven Limbs of Accumulation

1.1. *The limb of prostration*

1.1.1. *Synopsis*

> In the worlds however many they are of the ten directions,
> Are all the lions of men gone in the three times,
> I prostrate to all of them without exception,
> With admiring body, speech, and mind.

The phrase "however many" is plural in meaning. Thus, this line is speaking of the uncountably many world realms ***however many they are*** in the places endless as the limits of space are endless[27]. It is not

---

[27] The verse as shown is translated according to the commentary's explanation. However, the explanation and the translation with it are mistaken—the phrase "however many they are" has been joined to "the worlds in the ten directions" when in fact it joins to "all the lions of men gone in the three times". That the latter is correct can be seen immediately from the grammar of the verse and this is supported by all the Indian commentaries and by the original Tibetan commentary of Yeshe De who oversaw the official translation of the prayer into Tibetan. When the mistaken explanation arose amongst Tibetans is

(continued ...)

considering the world realms in any one direction or time but is considering the *world* realms *of the ten directions*—the four cardinal and four intermediate directions and the directions above and below—that is, boundless, limitless universes[28] of worlds.

Seated *in* those world realms are the buddhas of the three times, for example, in the case of this Endurance World field there are: the buddhas of the past Krakucchanda, Kanakamuni, and Kāśhyapa; the teacher of the present, the compassionate Śhākyamuni; and the buddhas of the future, from Maitreya the Guardian through the other nine hundred and ninety-seven who are intending to be buddhas here. The buddhas of the three times are the tathāgatas who, relying on the pleasant cause, the bodhisatva vehicle, *have gone*[29] to the pleasant fruition, the high rank of a complete buddha *in the three times*. With their supreme good qualities such as the

---

[27](... continued)
not known, but in this case Tenpa'i Wangchuk who passed away during the writing of this book inherited it from Adzom Gyalsay's commentary (20th century), which inherited it from Dza Patrul's commentary (19th century), which inherited it from Lochen Dharmashri's commentary (17th century). This incorrect explanation has now become universally accepted in Tibetan culture as the correct explanation. The problem is fully explained in my own commentary to this verse in volume I. The correct translation can be seen in the translation of the sutra earlier in this book.

[28] He has to make this explanation because the wording behind "world realms" is used in various ways in Sanskrit and Tibetan to signify various levels of cosmic reality. The author is making sure that the audience understands that "world realms" in this case does not mean, for instance, "planetary systems" or "galaxies" or "local galactic clusters" but means universes at a time, which are limitless in number according to the Buddha.

[29] Throughout the prayer, "*gone* in the three times" refers to the tathāgatas of the three times, because they are literally *the ones gone to suchness* or truly complete buddhahood in the three times.

set of twenty-one qualities of un-outflowed wisdom—the ten strengths, four non-fears, eighteen unmixed ones, and so on—they are like the king of beasts, the lion, who, when he lays claim to the snowy mountains, lords over the wild beasts there as a whole. Having no fear and anxiety, these ones who are supreme amongst humans are therefore called **lions of men**. To **all** of them, their number being uncountable, **I** the person who will make the prostration, **will prostrate to all of them** who are the object of prostration—the countless buddhas **without exception** seated in the boundless universes of field realms of the ten directions—**with** an utterly **admiring**[30] mind of faith that comes of knowing about them, through respectful **body**, respectful **speech, and** respectful **mind**.

1.1.2. Extended Explanation

1.1.2.1. Prostration through body

> Through the forces of excellent conduct prayer
> All conquerors are seen in direct perception by mind;
> Through utterly bowing with bodies many as the field atoms,
> I utterly prostrate to all the conquerors.

This prostration is done through having become familiar with meditation. All of the previous buddhas have for the sake of all the sentient beings pervading the limits of space aroused the excellent thought, the mind for supreme enlightenment, trained in the excellent conduct of the six pāramitās, and, in order in order to liberate all sentient beings of the three realms from the ocean of unsatisfactoriness have, at the time of the difficult activities of making an offering of head, limbs, and so on, made prayers like this: "If I pray that in the future when I am a buddha the various sentient beings will turn their attention to me, before long I will come in front of those sentient beings. At that time may I be able to protect

---

[30] This admiration is one of the three types of faith: admiring, longing, and trusting.

them from all their fears and problems!" **Through** or by the power of ***the forces*** of the oceans ***of excellent conduct prayers*** they have made like that, they have now finalized completing, ripening, and purifying[31], that is, they have gained the rank of a buddha and are continuously and without hindrance working for the sake of migrators by means of the two form bodies. Thus, if I now supplicate ***all*** the ***conquerors of the ten directions*** together with their sons equal in number to the field atoms while visualizing them as an object of ***mind***, they will come into direct sight in front of me, the supplicator and so ***seen in direct perception by mind***. Paying attention to me with their minds, looking on me with their eyes, listening to me with their ears, they will definitely be present there in front of me, a blind person, as though I had sight. It has been said like this:

> Someone who, imagining, turns his attention that way,
> Will have the Capable One present in front of him,[32]
> And he will be empowered and blessed.

And the great Orgyan said:

> For the faithful persons men and women ॰
> Padmasambhava lies at the door[33], never departing. ॰
> For my life, there is no death and departure. ॰
> In front of each faithful person, there is indeed a
>   Padmasambhava! ॰

---

[31] The Prajñāpāramitā teachings explain that a bodhisatva has three tasks which he must complete as he progresses to enlightenment: completing all of his prayers, ripening those who will be his disciples, and purifying meaning perfecting a buddha field for his disciples.

[32] For Capable One, see the glossary.

[33] This image comes from Tibetan society. Someone who belongs to a situation lies on the floor at the door, similar to a watchdog who is constantly there, constantly available and protecting the situation.

Thus, the object of prostration is the conquerors of the ten directions together with their sons who, present seated in the space in front of you, are to be visualized as present there. As well as that, you the person prostrating in front of them the accumulation-field object emanate this body of yours into bodies as many as the number of atoms of the fields of the ten directions, which is the unfathomable number of atoms that there would be if the fields which are the boundless, limitless universes of the ten directions were reduced to atoms. Then, all of the infinite sentient beings, yourself and others, single-mindedly think, "From today until gaining enlightenment we, with highly respectful three doors bow down with the utmost respect". **Through utterly bowing** down—meaning bowing down with the utmost respect—*with bodies* as **many as the field atoms utterly prostrate to all the conquerors**, the ones who have conquered the warring hordes of the four māras, the complete buddha bhagavats equal in number to the field atoms.

If the benefits to a person who in the past prostrated before a stupa containing the Buddha's relics were infinite, what could be said about the inconceivable benefit here where the object of prostration is the buddhas of the boundless, limitless universe fields of the ten directions and the person prostrating to them is prostrating with emanations equal to the count of the field atoms, a situation in which both the force of the compassionate activity and blessings of all the buddhas of the ten directions and the force of one's own faith and devotion have met?!

1.1.2.2. Prostration through mind

> On a single atom buddhas many as atoms
> Are seated at the centre of buddha sons;
> I imagine in that way that all the dharmadhātus
> Without exception are filled with conquerors.

This prostration is done through meeting the view. Those who have realized exactly as it is the actuality which is the dharmatā of all dharmas will be able to have something of this sort shine forth as an object of mind, whereas those who are other than that, individualized beings, will find it difficult to fit into their ordinary type of mind.

On a single atom are seated **buddhas** as **many** in number **as** however many **atoms** there are in the world realms. Their being seated there neither cramped nor thinly spread and without the atoms having increased in size nor the buddhas having decreased in size, is the dharmatā of things[34]. Moreover, they have a retinue of buddha sons. Using Buddha Śhākyamuni to illustrate this, there would be the three of his bodily son Rāhula, his speech sons the śhrāvakas and pratyekas, and his mind sons the bodhisatvas. Of them, the mind sons, the bodhisatvas, have the three special features of being: the ones who carry the family line of the conquerors; the ones who hold the treasury of holy dharma; and the ones who are to protect the ones yet to be tamed. In that way, there **are** buddhas **seated at the centre of** their surrounding **buddha sons** without being squeezed or cramped, and without interfering with or being mixed up with the others.

And **I imagine** that **in that way** exactly, they are also present in **all the** places[35] where space pervades and **dharmadhātu** pervades **without exception**. To give an example for this: buddhas equal to the number of field atoms on a single atom with their bodhisatva sons are there just like a sesame seed pod opened up[36]. Like that, I imagine that all those places where the dharmadhātu pervades, **are filled** without gaps **with conquerors** and their sons. Remembering their good qualities of body, speech, mind, qualities, and activity and

---

[34] For dharmatā, see the glossary. Here it means, "is the actual situation, how it really is, with things".

[35] "Places" here follows the plural form "dharmadhātus" seen in the verse.

[36] A sesame pod is packed with little seeds, but with every one of them in its own place and seemingly fitting in with all the others.

of their threefold knowledge, love, and capacity, then producing limitless faith and devotion towards them with your mind is referred to as "prostration by mind".

If you wonder, "How could that many buddhas—the ones equal to the number of atoms of the world realms—fit on a single atom?", it is something that does not fit into our ordinary type of rational mind but can be visible in the domain of the wisdom-mind of the buddhas and of the bodhisatvas with mastery. That is so because of the key point of all dharmas being interdependent. In other words, buddhas equal to the number of atoms in the world realms seated on top of a single atom can happen in the appearances of the pure ones[37] because of the key point that all dharmas are interdependent. It has been said like this:

> In interdependency, nothing could not work.
> In emptiness, nothing could not fit.

And:

> Anywhere that there could be emptiness,
> There, everything would be.
> Anywhere that there could not be emptiness,
> There, everything would not be.

Thus, because of the key point that within all phenomena there is not a single one that is truly established, any appearance of interdependency that could be can shine forth. If there were true existence, these appearances of interdependency would not shine forth. The fact that all phenomena are without truth is because the actuality of all phenomena is emptiness. Because of the key point of their being empty, the appearances of interdependency can shine forth in any

---

[37] The pure ones are those who have attained the path of seeing, the ones who see emptiness in direct perception, also called the noble ones. The impure ones are the ordinary sentient beings in samsara, the ones who have not reached that level of development, also called individualized beings.

way, in which case the appearance of buddhas as many as there are atoms on a single atom is workable. Because of the key point of their being interdependent, within all phenomena there is not so much as a single one that is not empty. That being the case, Ju Mipham said:

> If in the realm of knowables one were truly established,
> All this knowable would become absolutely non-apparent.
> Because not even one knowable is truly established
> The mode of phenomena as a limitless knowable is vividly
>   present.

If in the realm of knowables one of them was truly established, then this mode in which each one of the phenomena of the knowable is established as a thing of interdependency would not be able to happen. In the realm of knowables there is no true establishment, so these phenomena of the knowable can appear, can shine forth stoppagelessly as the superficies of interdependent origination. Appearances being interdependent in origination, they do not fall into any side whatsoever—if these appearances fell onto the side of purity, then these appearances of impurity could not shine forth; if these appearances fell onto the side of impurity, then these appearances of purity could not shine forth. That being so, it has to be said of these appearances that they "Do not fall onto any side either of purity or impurity". Thus it is necessary, given that appearances can shine forth and can shine forth without stoppage—the key point of interdependency—and given that there is not so much as a single truly-established appearance within these appearances of interdependency—the key point of emptiness—these two points of being empty and interdependent are joined as a pair. Thus, the presence on a single atom of buddhas as many as there are atoms happens because of the two key points of it being interdependency and being the dharmatā of things.

It is like in the past Jetsun Mila sat inside a yak horn without him growing smaller or the yak horn growing bigger and like in the past Jowo Je, the unequalled Dīpaṃkara, seated himself inside a clay mould without the mould growing larger or himself growing smaller and said:

> If philosophers try to understand this, it will not sit well with their rational minds, but having gone around both India and Tibet they could swear an oath that this is what the actuality of all phenomena is like!

1.1.2.3. Prostration through speech

> Those oceans of unending commendation
> Have using all sounds of the ocean of aspects of the voice
> The good qualities of all the conquerors utterly expressed
> And I praise all of the ones gone to bliss.

Those buddhas of the ten directions and three times together with their bodhisatva assemblies have inconceivable good qualities—for example, the miracles of body, teachings of speech, and fully expressing mind. Having recalled their good qualities, those buddhas are referred to as having good qualities worthy of ***commendation*** or praise. When making such praise, it is not done with merely this one body of yours but with unfathomable bodies equal in number to the field atoms. On those unfathomable bodies are unfathomable heads and in those unfathomable heads are unfathomable tongues and palates, and it is through possession of these three or four unfathomable items that the ***ocean of unending*** good qualities of buddhahood are expressed.

The mode of the praise is that it is intoned ***using all*** the various different vocal ***sounds*** equal in number to the drops of water comprising ***the ocean of*** or unending ***aspects of the voice***[38] of enlightenment which are likened to the sweet-sounding, measured, and complex patterns of rhythm in the intonation of Brahma's speech.

---

[38] "The voice" is the voice of enlightenment as is comes out in the speech of the buddhas.

In that way, commendation for *the* many **good qualities** of the inconceivable three secrets³⁹—such as the ten strengths, four non-fears, eighteen unmixed ones, set of twenty-one good qualities of un-outflowed wisdom, thirty-seven dharmas of the side of enlightenment, and so on—*of all* without exception of *the conquerors* equal to the world realms is utterly expressed. It says, "utterly expressed", but when an attempt is made to express the good qualities of buddhahood, they are found to be beyond limit. For example, when glorious Chandrakīrti expresses the good qualities of buddhahood in his *Entering the Middle Way*, he says that there is no end to them and if he with his powerful intellect was not able to express them except for saying just that, how could there be an end to them? As an example of how this expression of the endless qualities of buddhahood proceeds, I have been taught that it is like a bird flying in the sky—there is no end to the sky, so, when its wings are exhausted, the bird simply drops back to the ground. Thus, expressing the good qualities of the three secrets of the buddhas, "*I* with great respect **praise all of the ones gone to bliss**⁴⁰ together with their sons".⁴¹

Even if the qualities of buddhahood were expressed for one hundred thousand aeons by bodhisatvas who had attained the levels, the task would not be finished. Nevertheless, there is benefit in making a praise even one time: previously, during the time our teacher was on the path of training, the buddha named "Kalgyal" passed away and set himself in equipoise on the fire samādhi; at that time our teacher

---

³⁹ For three secrets, see the glossary.

⁴⁰ "Ones gone to bliss" is a translation of the Sanskrit "sugatas".

⁴¹ There are two ways of understanding this verse according to Indian commentaries. Here he has explained one of them because of following Adzom Gyalsay's commentary in which the praise of the fourth line has been accomplished through the praise of the third line. The two ways of understanding the verse are clearly explained in my own commentary on this verse, which includes Adzom Gyalsay's entire commentary to verse.

went before him and, lifting up one leg and placing it on top of his head[42], said:

> Foremost among beings! Other great spiritual trainees
>   like you do not exist in the god levels
> Nor do they exist in the supreme places, the palaces of the
>   gods that do not exist in this world.
> Where could one like you exist even in the vast area above
>   the ground with its mountains and their forest tracts?

In saying that one verse a vast accumulation equivalent to one made during many aeons was completed. So, if you imagine that all the buddhas of the three times and ten directions are seated in the space before you, and think that you make many emanations of your body before them, emanations which then continuously make praises to the buddhas' three secrets of body, speech, and mind, an accumulation of many aeons will definitely be completed and obscurations definitely will be purified.

1.2. The limb of making offerings

1.2.1. Surpassable offering

> I will make offerings to those conquerors
> With the finest flowers, finest garlands,
> Small cymbals, ointments, supreme parasols,
> Supreme oil lamps, and finest incense.

> I will make offerings to those conquerors
> With the finest clothes, supreme scents,
> And mixed powders equal to Mt. Meru,
> And all with the best of excellent displays.

You think that you ***will make offerings to those conquerors with the finest flowers*** of the human world both the artificial ones and the

---

[42] "Our teacher" is Śhākyamuni Buddha. His former incarnation placed his leg up on top of his own head, which was a way of highly respectful salutation.

non-artificial ones that grow in water and in the fields, all of which are visually beautiful in their white, yellow, red, green, and other colours that capture the eye and their visual forms that delight the mind, are fragrant to smell, sweet to taste, and soft to touch, and all in various nice arrangements. And in the gods' worlds there are the Mañjughoṣha, Great Mañjughoṣha, and so on flowers beautifying the entire area of the ground of those field realms and also strewn in a carpet specifically across Lovely to Behold[43] and there is also a great rain of various flowers delightful, beautiful, and lovely descending from the sky, and you think that you are offering all of those. And as well, "finest" here means that you think that you are making offerings of various flowers arising from the buddhas and bodhisatvas' samādhis, prayers, and arousings of mind—lotuses, great lotuses, utpala, udumbara, puṇḍarīka[44], and so on, so beautiful and lovely that you cannot get enough of seeing them.

"*Finest garlands*" means that you think that you are offering garlands strung from the precious substances whose value is beyond estimation, like the seven precious substances of gold, silver, yellow sapphire, white sapphire, blue sapphire, and so on. Moreover, you think you are making an offering to adorn the places where the unadorned nirmāṇakāyas are seated, their immeasurable palaces, and so on, and are making an offering such as "the five silk garments and the eight ornaments of precious substance" to adorn the bodies of the adorned saṃbhogakāyas.

"*Small cymbals*" means an offering of inconceivable types of musical instruments which when played bring joy to the ears—the threefold blown, struck, and clashed instruments consisting of bells, lutes,

---

[43] Mañjughoṣha and Great Mañjughoṣha are ravishingly beautiful flowers found in the desire god realms. Lovely to Behold is the main city of the gods of the Thirty-Three Heaven near the top of the desire realm.

[44] These are different varieties of the lotus flower.

flutes, small cymbals, and so on whose sounds are pleasing to the ear and delightful.

"*Ointments*" means that you imagine an offering to the conquerors of many different types of those fragrant substances made suitable for rubbing onto the body, whether of one simple or a complex smell—for example, red and white Sandalwood, Aloe, Camphor, Saffron, the six excellent medicinals[45], and so on.

"*Supreme parasols*" means offering various white parasols, with gold handles, that alleviate the suffering of heat. Furthermore, "supreme parasols" is an offering made by many gods and goddesses which you have emanated of parasols made from various precious substances that are so beautiful and lovely that one never has enough of seeing them, with each of the gods and goddesses holding an umbrella over the head of each of the buddhas, and in addition, an offering of umbrellas which appear from space to sit unsupported above the conquerors' heads.

"*Supreme lamps*" means offerings made with the following types of light: from actual oil lamps which are various containers made from precious substances such as gold and silver, and also the five and seven types of precious substance, and so on, filled with grain or vegetable oils; and from supreme lamps which are the naturally-occurring lamps such as the sun, moon, and so on; and from lamps which are the various types of precious jewels whose light rays are able to illuminate all the third order worlds; and especially from the supreme of lamps, prajñā lamps or dharma lamps, given that their light is what dispels the darkness of the delusion of ignorance.

"*Finest incense*" is the offering of incense of one simple smell like that made only from the Aloe called "elephant essence" or from the

---

[45] The six excellent medicinals are: nutmeg, bamboo juice, saffron, cloves, cardamom meaning cardamom with the small seed pods, and kakola meaning cardamom with large seed pods.

Sandalwood called "snake essence", and similarly of incense of complex smell, that is, incense made by compounding many differing fragrant substances such as Sandalwood, Camphor, Aloe, and so on. And especially, "finest incense" is to offer the smell of pure discipline or the excellent smell of completely pure discipline.

With those sorts of offering things, *I will* perpetually *make offerings* with highly respectful three doors *to* the object of offering, *those conquerors* equal in number to the atoms of fields of the ten directions together with their sons.

I will make offerings with the "*finest clothes*" meaning clothing made of godly substances of inexpressible value. Fine clothing is described as "finely-woven, soft, light, divine clothing" meaning clothing that to begin with is finely woven, then is soft to the touch, and finally is light in weight—it is clothing with many special features. Such clothing is imagined to be offered to the nirmāṇakāyas, appearing as they do without adornments, in the form of the three dharma robes offered for example to Buddha Śākyamuni, and offered to the saṃbhogakāyas, appearing as they do with adornments, in the form of the five silk garments offered for example to Vajrasatva.

"*Supreme scents*" are liquid compounds of various excellent fragrances such as the six excellent fragrances, the twelve excellent fragrances, and so on, that are first used to sprinkle an entire area so that dust will not arise from it then used to set out many water offerings of excellent smell in an amazing presentation.

And I will make offerings *with mixed powders*. "Mixed powders" refers to mixtures of various good-smelling incense powders which could be divided up and burned to give off a scent but which instead have been into bundled into packages inside five-coloured silks. You must think that you heap together many such packages of mixed powders until they are *equal* in size *to* the king of mountains **Mt. Meru**, then offer them.⁴⁶

Moreover, those offering substances mentioned above are, as expressed in the saying "excellent things of highest quality in a good display", imagined to be *in the* form of the ***best of excellent displays***, which, if illustrated using just one of those types of offering, such as flowers, is to imagine them in the form of parasols made of flowers, victory banners of flowers, the eight auspicious signs made of flowers, the eight substances made of flowers, the seven precious substances made of flowers, immeasurable palaces made of flowers, thrones made of flowers, and so on. And then with all of those inconceivable clouds of offerings in the best of displays, I will make offerings to the object of offering, all those conquerors with their sons.

Similarly, there is the mode of offering in which the displays in this third-order world system are viewed as an offering, with a good display, of the five desirables. According to what Patrul Rinpoche said:

> If you imagine then offer like this, there will be inconceivable benefits:

---

⁴⁶ Tib. phur ma. "Mixed powders" in the ancient Indian context of the prayer referred to individual ingredients of incense which had been powdered, mixed, and piled high, usually in urns. In India, it was popular to put vessels piled with mixed incense powders like this into a room in order to provide a fragrance to the room. In Tibet the same thing was done but the handfuls of the powder were sewn into cloth wrappings first, which is why the author explains it this way—it is similar to the European idea of lavender bags and the like. Commentaries by Indian authors do not talk about powders that have been mixed and wrapped into packages in silks or other fine materials because this was a Tibetan form which did not exist in India when this prayer was composed.

East, the lamps of the sun and moon,
South, the incense of sandalwood forests,
West, the godly foods of white and red snows,
North, the offering waters of the blue Dzachu river[47].
Below, the flowers of precious gold,
Above, the music of the turquoise-blue dragon ...

1.2.2. Unsurpassable offering

Generally speaking, the meaning of "unsurpassable offering" is as follows. The sort of offering which is manifested through the buddhas and bodhisatvas' samādhi, prayer, and arousing of mind is matchless within the extent of becoming, there being no offering better that could be found, so it is referred to "unsurpassable offering".

> The offerings which are unsurpassed, vaster,
> Those are also imagined for all the conquerors;
> Through the forces of faith in excellent conduct
> I will prostrate and offer to all the conquerors.

The offerings which are purer, vaster in extent, better displayed, ***unsurpassed*** or unexceeded, the offering clouds of wish-granting cows, wish-fulfilling trees, wish-fulfilling gems, unfathomable offering goddesses of charm, garlands, song, dance, and so on arising from the displays of the samādhis and miracles of the buddhas and of the bodhisatvas with mastery are, being like the articles of the space store, a ***vaster*** sort of offering. It has been taught that this type of offering requires being done at the fictional level through special methods such as the manifestations of Samantabhadra and at the superfactual level through no referencing of the three spheres—the three of that being offered, the action of offering, and the agent performing the offering.

---

[47] Dzachu River is a river near the town Dzachuka, from which Patrul gets his name "Dza Patrul".

Similarly, arousing the mind for supreme enlightenment, retaining dharma through non-forgetfulness, and practising in accordance with the profound meaning are also taught in sutra as "the unsurpassed offering"[48].

In regard to that, to someone who says, "The offering using the goddesses of the desirables—Charm and the others—does not fit with the sutra tradition", Adzom Gyalsay in his commentary written according to the oral tradition of Patrul Rinpoche replies, "Well, the *Avataṃsaka Sutra* states that many sons and daughters of the gods made offerings to the bhagavat, therefore, your reasoning that an offering of the eight goddesses, Charm and the others, does not fit with the sutra tradition is unfounded".

Those clouds of offerings made in these modes of offering—the surpassed and unsurpassed offerings stated in the verse lines immediately above[49]—***are***, having ***again*** thought of the immeasurable good qualities of the conquerors with devotion and faith and respect, offered ***to all the conquerors***.[50]

---

[48] This is derived from the explanation given in Yeshe De's commentary, where he points out that the Buddha, in a specific sutra, explains that there are three types of offerings that are pure like the god Brahmā is pure. Of the three, the unsurpassed one is to carry out the three things just explained.

[49] Tenpa'i Wangchuk explains here that "those" refers to both the surpassed and unsurpassed offerings but the Indian commentaries, Yeshe De, and even Adzom Gyalway on whom Tenpa'i Wangchuk bases his explanation, clearly state that these two lines are only about the unsurpassed offering, with "those" referring only to the unsurpassed offering. I feel sure that Tenpa'i Wangchuk was presenting this more comprehensive understanding in order to generate enthusiasm for practice in the lay people to whom this commentary was first given.

[50] Tenpa'i Wangchuk's explanation gives a meaning for this line which
(continued ...)

Contemplating the certainty that there will be unfathomable benefits if I train in the excellent conduct—which starts with arousing the excellent thought of the mind for supreme enlightenment and is followed by performing the excellent conduct of the conduct of enlightenment, which, consisting of the six pāramitās, includes doing prostrations, making offerings, and so on—the forces of trusting faith are aroused. ***Through*** being motivated by ***the forces of*** trusting ***faith in*** the ***excellent conduct***, here ***I will*** by combining both the limb of prostration and the limb of offering as explained earlier ***prostrate and offer to*** the object having special features—***all the conquerors***.

An additional point is that, when there is trusting faith, the buddhas' blessings can enter anywhere—things like the old woman calling a dog's tooth the Buddha's tooth can happen. Also, the great Orgyan said:

> Through trusting faith blessings enter.
> If you free your mind of doubt, your wishes will be accomplished.

That being so, it is important not to doubt what is being discussed here with thoughts like, "Is there any benefit to it when I offer something like one prostration or a small lamp?" Given that the object involved is a buddha—an object having special features—even offering something as small as a single bean has unfathomable benefit. The Buddha explained that previously he was a Wheel-Wielding King named "Suckle On Me" who governed four continents and had sufficient power over the gods of the Heaven of the Thirty-Three to share the throne of their leader Kauśhika equally with him, which was the result of previously having made offerings of seven beans to a buddha named "bsod skyabs".

---

[50](... continued)
differs a little from the wording seen in the verse. This is not surprising given that the wording of this line in the verse is explained in several different ways even in the Indian commentaries.

1.3. The limb of laying aside evil

> Under the influence of desire, anger, and delusion
> And through body, speech, and likewise mind,
> The evils I have done whichever they might be,
> I lay all of them aside, each one individually.

Generally speaking, there is not a single non-virtuous evil deed that is not caused by the three poisons. As has been said:

> When it has been created from one of the three
> Desire, anger, and delusion, it is non-virtue.

Thus, evil which is to be laid aside has its cause in the three poisons, that is, it has been created **under the influence of** being motivated by one or more of **desire, anger, and delusion. And** the ones who accumulate the evil—myself and all other sentient beings—have been accumulating it since beginningless samsara **through** the ten non-virtues of **body**—the three of killing, taking what has not been given, and unclean behaviour[51]—and **speech**—the four of lying, divisive speech, coarse speech, and gossip—**and likewise mind**—the three of covetous mind, harmful mind, and wrong views. And through the five immediates, the five close to them, the four heavy ones, and the eight wrongs. And outwardly through the transgressions of the vows of personal emancipation; inwardly through the transgressions of the bodhisatva trainings; and secretly through the transgressions of the vidyādhara mantra samayas. And through abjuring worldly oaths, and through loss of both personal shame and sense of propriety, and through natural downfalls and downfalls with associated a vow, and so on. Of all the evils that I have done, there are the ones I have done myself, the ones I have caused others to do, and the ones I have rejoiced in others doing. These **evils I have done whichever they might be**, while not keeping them secret and

---

[51] "Unclean behaviour" refers to sexual behaviour. For monks and nuns it means engaging in sex, for lay people it means engaging in improper sex.

not hiding them, and with intense remorse and regret, *I lay all of them aside, each one individually*.

We ordinary beings—which excludes everyone who, having reached the level of a noble one and gained mastery, has come into the world realms according his own intentions to work for the sake of migrator sentient beings—definitely have since the beginninglessness of samsara accumulated a large amount of non-virtuous evil karma—high as a mountain, deep as an ocean—that will be experienced in this life, experienced in other ones, and so on. That being the case, there is laying aside to be done.

When doing laying aside, it is important to actually bring to mind all non-virtues that we can remember. For all the rest that we cannot remember, how could there be anything not seen by the wisdom eye of the conquerors and their sons? Thus, thinking that one is in sight of the conquerors and their sons, it is important to do the laying aside with a complete set of the four forces of antidote and from the depths of your heart.

In particular, as part of relying on the force of rejection[52], it is good to tell others the extent of the evil you have done. It is as Patrul says:

> The more evil you have done,
> The more other beings you should tell about it.

Therefore, he says:

> That evil if told to others goes on to be purified. Virtue told to others goes on to be exhausted.

---

[52] The force of rejection is one of the four forces of the antidote. It is the force of rejecting the bad action because of understanding that it belongs to the first two of the four truths, that is because of developing the understanding that it is part of samsaric suffering.

Then, if you lay evil aside from your heart and do so with intense regret, it can be purified. And especially, if enlightenment mind and the view of emptiness are aroused together in your mindstream, evil deeds and downfalls can be totally purified. Even if your efforts do not totally purify the evil, it will not need to be experienced except as small ripening. Previously a bhikṣhu of the noble land, India, who was a great holder of the Vinaya, committed the first of the four defeats after which he did much laying aside in which he relied only on taking refuge with deep regret. At the time of his death, he fell into hell because of that defeat. At that time, the henchmen of the Lord of Death raised their various weapons and came at him saying, "You are a person who has corrupted his discipline because of which you are about to experience suffering in this place for many aeons". He was terrified. At the very moment the henchmen pounced on him to kill him, he made a supplication to the Three Jewels. After death, he was born immediately in the god's abode, the Heaven of the Thirty Three. This is how it is then: although he had not been able to totally purify the evil and it ripened as birth in hell, he only had to experience it as though being struck by a ball of silk and did not need to experience it for more than the blink of an eye.

Similarly, there is the point that if laying aside has been done, there can be total purification of the ripening involved. Again there was a bhikṣhu of the noble land, India, a holder of the Vinaya who, because of defeat, had a downfall of vows. Having deep regret for it, he did nothing but laying it aside. At some point in time, he experienced omens of having really purified the evil in various dreams. One day, when he had gone travelling, he reached a large river which had to be crossed. He entered a boat and was ready to go when he met with a dharma friend from before who said, "It is not all right for we two to be together in the boat. You are a person who was lax with your vows, so it is not all right to be connected with you and your food[53]". He stated, "I am a person who was lax with his

---

[53] It is regarded that one should not eat food with nor drink from the
(continued ...)

vows but, having done laying aside, the evil downfalls have been totally purified". The other said, "Well then, what do you have to show that the evil was in truth purified?" He stated, "If my evil downfalls have been purified, may my feet not come into contact with the water and so may I cross this river! If they have not been purified, may I drown in the river!" With that declaration that it was true, it went as he said and, his feet not coming into contact with the water, he crossed the river.

That being so, no matter what evils we have done, it is extremely important to lay them aside! These days when we say, "I did something bad", we judge it merely according to the outer, worldly sense of it. For example, if a bhikshu slaughters one hundred yaks, that will indeed be judged as an extreme evil[54] and, henceforth, people will ask how even the name bhikṣhu could be given to him. However, if one has a bad mind towards a bodhisatva and it leads to a physical show of dislike, no one will think that an evil has been done, yet as Chagmey Rinpoche said:

> A greater evil than killing the sentient beings of the three worlds
> Is to denigrate the bodhisatvas.

Leave aside killing the sentient beings of the three realms, if you kill one hundred men, how could you go up to emancipation with that? Furthermore, in the sutras it says that, compared to glaring at the sentient beings of the three realms, it is worse to look badly at one bodhisatva. That being the case, if, without examining your own mindstream, you think "I am without evil deeds", but in fact have ones that are great evils, you are downplaying and underestimating what you are accumulating. For example, deprecating others might be a very small bad thing in the context of the personal emancipation

---

[53](... continued)
same water source as a person who has corrupted his vows.

[54] ... because yaks are extremely valuable for Tibetans.

or bodhisatva vows, but is a root downfall which transgresses the command of the sugata in the context of secret mantra.

In short, it is important not to become shrouded with evil to begin with. However, if you fall into doing something evil, it is definitely important to restore yourself by laying that evil aside via the four forces of the antidote.

1.4. The limb of rejoicing

> I rejoice in all merits whoever has them,
> Those of all the conquerors of the ten directions and
> The buddha sons, of the pratyekabuddhas, of those
> In training and not in training, and of all migrators.

I rejoice in all of the roots of virtue ***whoever has them***, such as ***those of all the conquerors***, the complete buddhas, seated in the boundless, limitless universes ***of the ten directions***, merits that have come from having trained in the bodhisatva's conduct, ***and*** those of ***the buddha sons***, the bodhisatvas having the three special features of being the ones who carry the family line of the conquerors, the ones who hold the treasury of holy dharma, and the ones who are able to protect the remaining ones to be tamed. And I rejoice in those ***of the pratyekabuddhas***, the ones who have achieved the rank of self-made conqueror through the meditation which by the condition of watching charnel ground corpses has reversed the forward order of the twelve links of interdependency. And I rejoice in those ***of*** the speech sons, the śrāvaka saṅgha, comprised of the śrāvaka trainees referred to as ***"those in training"***—the three of stream-enterer, returner, and non-returner—***and*** the śrāvakas who have achieved the rank of arhat, referred to as ***not in training***. ***And***, I rejoice with an utterly joyful mind in the entire extent ***of*** merits accumulated by ***all migrators***, the ordinary individualized beings who have not even entered the paths of accumulation and merit.

In short, I will, with the great joy that comes from a mind without jealousy, rejoice in all of them—the outflowed virtues of ordinary beings, the roots of virtue of the two accumulations of those who have entered the paths of the three vehicles, and the roots of virtue of the tremendous deeds done for others' sakes at the time of the buddhas' twelve deeds.

When you see others making tremendous virtue because of developing the cause for enlightenment, the two accumulations, if you rejoice in it with the same joy as you would have if you were making that virtue yourself, the roots of merit you gain are equal to that gained by the other. Chagmey Rinpoche said:

> If when you hear of another's creation of virtue,
> You abandon the non-virtuous mind of jealousy over it,
> And rejoice in it from your heart with joy,
> That will result in gaining equal merit, it was taught[55].

And:

> Contemplating the fact that it is a small hardship
> For great meaning, be earnest in your rejoicing!

And:

> You could weigh the third-order world on a beam scale the size of Mt. Meru,
> But the roots of virtue come from rejoicing are not like that.

Furthermore, it is like in the historical event recounted in the sutras in which King Prasenajit, having planned for a grand dharma teaching, invited the Buddha and his retinue, and while the king was creating a tremendous amount of virtue by making offerings etcetera to them as a welcoming gesture, the poor woman Dead Bamboo rejoiced in what he was doing[56]. Thus, the roots of merit made

---

[55] ... by the Buddha.

[56] ... and the Buddha explained to the king afterwards that the poor woman had accumulated more merit than anyone of the king and his
(continued ...)

through rejoicing are more than tremendous. The roots of merit of a bodhisatva noble one would be hard for us ordinary beings to gain, but if we rejoice in the various roots of merit of another ordinary being comparable to ourselves, then we will definitely gain them ourselves.

1.5. The limb of urging to turn the dharma wheel

> Ones who are lamps of the worlds of the ten directions
> Have become buddhas at the enlightenment stage and
>   gained the undefiled state;
> I urge all of those guardians
> To turn the unsurpassed wheel.

"*The ones who*" is a plural pronoun referring to the ones who *are the lamps* or great sources of illumination that dispel the darkness of the ignorance *of the worlds of the ten directions*. They are the ones who, when they were on the path of training before they had become complete buddhas, went step by step *through the stages* of the ten levels and five paths so as to obtain the rank of *enlightenment* or buddhahood[57]. They have *gained* the rank of manifest *buddhahood* which, because afflictions have been abandoned, has the capacity to remain *undefiled* in regard to all the dharmas of the knowable. For them, all obscurations to the knowable having been abandoned, all dharmas are known without obstruction, like putting a moistened Emblic Myrobalan in the palm of the hand. Thus, they

---

[56](... continued)
retinue because of her pure-minded rejoicing in the activities of the event.

[57] The correct wording for this line is shown in the verse above. A mistaken tradition of explanation of the words appeared in Tibet several or more centuries ago. The mistaken explanation, which is now universal amongst Tibetans, is seen in this sentence. This wording and with it a mistaken explanation appears in three places in the prayer. The line is fully explained in Nāgārjuna's and my own commentary in volume I.

have the attainment of the rank of buddha that has no obstructing defilement, yet, in order to expose the greatness of the holy dharma, they remain present while showing the mode of not teaching the dharma. Buddhas are called "guardians of the world". Thinking of those guardians who are not teaching the dharma, I emanate bodies equal in number to as many atoms as are in the fields, their hands holding a white dharma conch with clockwise whorls and a thousand-spoked golden wheel, and also the auspiciousness substances, the auspicious signs, the seven items of rulership of a king, and so on—items equal to the articles of Samantabhadra's manifested offerings and the space store. Then I make a supplication in which *I urge all of those guardian* buddhas, *to turn* uninterruptedly *the unsurpassed wheel* of the holy dharma consisting of the authentic statement and realization of the profound and vast.

Moreover, the learned and accomplished Karma Chagmey said:

> I urge the ones in all the universe worlds of the ten directions,
> Who, having become complete buddhas, have for a long time not done so,
> To turn the dharma wheel
> Quickly and in a vast way.
> Please know this through your mind with its extra-perceptions.

Previously, on reaching buddhahood, the Buddha Bhagavat showed the mode of not teaching dharma for seven weeks. After that, the leaders of the gods Brahmā and Kauśhika offered a white dharma conch with clockwise whorls and a thousand-spoked golden wheel and then supplicated the Buddha, and because of that the Buddha turned the first dharma wheel of the four truths. With that as an example, we in the present offer a maṇḍala of whatever we have in front of the gurus, the spiritual friends, then petition them to turn each of the dharma wheels. It has been taught that, if we are able to do that, there will be immeasurable benefits—a rain of holy dharma will fall in that region that will benefit many sentient beings, the karmic obscurations of having abandoned dharma will be purified, and so on.

1.6. The limb of supplicating to remain, not passing into nirvana

> I also will supplicate with my palms joined together those
> Who have asserted they will show passage into nirvana
> To stay for aeons as many as the field atoms.
> In order to bring benefit and ease to all migrators.

I, the person who is making the supplication *also will*, as was done in the last verse, *supplicate*. The way that I will offer the supplication will be *with* respectful body of *my palms* being *joined together*, with respectful speech of offering the supplication to stay, and with respectful mind of having aspiring, admiring, and trusting faiths. The supplication will be made "to whoever of *those* buddhas and bodhisatvas *who have asserted* that *they will show* the deed of *passage into nirvana*".

Generally speaking, the buddhas have already separated from the five aggregates with outflows, because of which they have transcended body and take no further samsaric birth. However, they do perform the final deed in which they show passage into nirvana in order to urge the minds of those with the characteristics of ones to be tamed towards dharma. That final deed is shown when working for the sakes of migrators in that realm has been completed. As well as that, some gurus, spiritual friends, and bodhisatvas show passage into nirvana in order to show disappointment with others who have been doing wrong practices.

Therefore, within their view and with emanations of this body of mine equal in number to the field atoms, I supplicate them not to pass into nirvana but *to stay for* a count of great *aeons as many as the atoms*[58] in the *field* of this Endurance World *in order to bring*

---

[58] A great aeon is the length of time approximately speaking of the
(continued ...)

the ultimate *benefit* of the rank of buddha *and* the temporary *ease* of protection from all the fears of samsara and the bad migrations *to* myself and others, *all migrators*. Note that "benefit and ease" can be taken in the way that is universally-known and is explained as "temporary benefit and a ultimate ease", but Adzom Gyalsay's commentary says that the words here should be understood in the reverse way according to the oral tradition of the Glorious King.[59]

One purpose for this supplication is that, if you supplicate the buddhas and bodhisatvas not to pass into nirvana, all of your karmic obscurations for a short life will be purified into having no remainder of body.

1.7. The limb of dedicating all roots of virtue to enlightenment

> I dedicate every trifle of virtue which
> I have accumulated in prostrating, offering,
> Laying aside, rejoicing, urging, and supplicating
> For the purpose of enlightenment.

The dedication of the roots of virtue of the above six limbs of accumulation are done together here. The six are: *prostrating* to the holy objects, the buddhas and bodhisatvas equal in number to the field atoms; making an *offering* with vast offerings of clouds of the surpassable and unsurpassable offerings; *laying aside* all the bad things which have been accumulated—both those made in connection with having a vow and not; *rejoicing* in all of the roots of virtue accumulated in the world realms; *urging* the all the buddhas and bodhisatvas to turn the dharma wheel; and *supplicating* all the

---

[58](... continued)
duration of a universe like ours.

[59] Benefit and ease usually means temporary benefit in samsara and the ultimate benefit of nirvana. Tenpa'i Wangchuk points this out because he is following the way that Dza Patrul, also known as "The Glorious King", explains it as recorded in Adzom Gyalsay's commentary.

buddhas and bodhisatvas who have asserted that they will pass into nirvana not to pass into nirvana.

The root of virtue connected with each one is a mere ***trifle of virtue*** similar to that created when a little monk offers a morsel of food to a single crow. I dedicate every bit of this virtue that ***I have accumulated*** by taking up the enlightenment mind and the prajñā realizing emptiness then dedicating it ***for the purpose of*** all the sentient beings pervading space gaining the rank of the great complete ***enlightenment*** in which there is no abiding in either of the two extremes.

The *Ornament of Manifest Realizations* says:

> Arousing the mind is wanting truly complete
> Enlightenment for others' sakes.

According to that text, if you have dedicated through having taken up the two sides or aspects of the enlightenment mind—fictional and superfactual enlightenment mind—the roots of merit involved are endless, which has been said like this:

> Just as a drop of water fallen into the water of an ocean
> Does not end for as long as the ocean does not end,
> Likewise virtue which has been wholly dedicated to
>   enlightenment also
> Does not come to an end until enlightenment has been
>   attained.

Not only that, I have been taught that even though a root of virtue might be small, if you have dedicated it to sentient beings, it is impossible for those objects of dedication not to get it: it is the power of the buddha's power, the force of truth of dharmatā, and your own excellent special intention[60].

---

[60] For special intention, see the glossary.

Generally speaking, even though you have made various karmas of white dharmas—the gathering of the accumulations, the purification of obscurations, and so on—it is exceptionally important, a burning issue, that you must join it with completely pure dedications and prayers.

In our lives we might have good, conducive conditions with effortless accomplishment of our wishes, no obstacles standing in the way, and so on, but we also have non-virtuous karmas accumulated from beginningless samsara, some of which will be experienced in this life and some in later lives, which means that we also have many karmas that can turn into obstacles for our accomplishment of dharma. Therefore, we need to judge ourselves according to how much we have gathered the accumulations and purified the obscurations and then with that must make completely pure prayers again and again. If we do not do that, it will be easy for us to fall under the control of karmas of evil accumulated in previous lives because they are more in number, greater in amount accumulated, and have been worked at during a longer period, and then there will be many occasions on which we enter wrong paths against our wishes.

For example, there are holy beings who received prophecies in an earlier life that they will be tulkus in the future. The emanations who have now been recognized as their tulkus are seen to have amazing qualities of learning, virtues, and attainment, so are like part of a chain of golden mountains of learned and accomplished beings. Even then, though, one still has to think "What obstacle could befall them in this life?" Therefore, so as not to meet obstacles of that sort, it is exceptionally important to make completely pure prayers of aspiration.

In gaining the rank of a buddha, if one has to pass through one life after another for many lives, even though some lives might be joyful and good, not to have obstacles to the holy dharma in any of them is difficult. Therefore, set supplicating the guru and Three Jewels, entrusting the activities to the dharma protectors and guards who protect the white side, and gathering the accumulations and purifying the obscurations as your judge and with that it is extremely important to make completely pure prayers.

2. An Extensive Explanation of the Divisions of the Actual Prayer

2.1. The Main Part

This has sixteen main topics:

> Pure thought, not forgetting enlightenment mind,
> Uncloaked conduct, benefit and ease,
> Armour, companions of same lot,
> Attending virtuous friends, making the tathāgatas visible,
> Holding holy dharma, acquiring a store,
> Entering, force, accomplishing, activity,
> Training following, and conclusion to it all.

The meaning is as follows. 1) "*Pure thought*" is prayer made for pure thought. 2) "*Not forgetting enlightenment mind*" is prayer made so as not to forget the enlightenment mind. 3) "*Uncloaked conduct*" is prayer for conduct which is uncloaked or undefiled. 4) "*Benefit and ease*" is prayer for setting sentient beings in benefit and ease. 5) "*Armour*" is prayer to be wearing armour. 6) "*Companions of same lot*" is prayer to have the company of friends of the same lot or type. 7) "*Attending virtuous friends*" is prayer for attending virtuous spiritual friends and pleasing them. 8) This is prayer for "*making the tathāgatas visible*". 9) This is prayer for wholly *holding* the *holy dharma*. 10) "*Acquiring a store*" is prayer for acquiring an unending store. 11) "*Entering*" is prayer for entering the conduct in many different ways. 12) "*Forces*" is prayer for the forces of enlightenment. 13) This is prayer made for *accomplishing* due to having the antidotes. 14) "*Activity*" is prayer for enlightened activity. 15) "*Training following*" is prayer to train following great beings. 16) "*Conclusion*" is concluding dedications to all of it.

2.1.1. Prayer for pure thought

This has four parts. There is prayer: for offering to the buddhas; to wholly fulfill the intent; to purify a buddha-field; and to benefit sentient beings.

2.1.1.1. Prayer for offering to the buddhas

> May I offer to the past buddhas and the ones
> Who are seated in the worlds of the ten directions.

There are the past buddhas Krakucchandha, Kanakamuni, and Kāshyapa of the one thousand and two buddhas of this good aeon, the Seven Successive Buddhas preceding them, and all the remaining countless buddhas who have descended in past aeons. And there are the present buddhas residing in the world realms of the ten directions—Buddha Vajrasatva in the eastern Abhirati Field, Buddha Ratnasaṃbhava of the southern Shrīmat Field, Buddha Amitābha in the western Stacked Lotuses Field, Buddha Amitābha in the northern Sukarmapurna Field, Buddha Vairochana in the central Ghanavyūha Field, and so on. In front of all of them, *may I*, having emanated my own body into bodies equal in number to the field atoms, all of whom are carrying unfathomable offering substances in their hands like the offering clouds of Samantabhadra, ***offer to the*** uncountable ***past buddhas and*** present buddhas, ***the ones who are seated in the*** unfathomable ***worlds of the ten directions***.

2.1.1.2. Prayer to wholly fulfill the intent

> Those whoever have not descended, most quickly
>   completing your intentions
> Descend to buddhahood at the enlightenment stage!

This is a prayer saying "May the persons who in the future will become buddhas, that is, the ones who will definitely attain buddhahood, the bodhisatvas who now are seated on the high levels, be able to wholly fulfil all of what they have asserted they will do. The "whoever" on the first line is part of the plural construction meaning "***those*** buddhas ***whoever*** they are who still ***have not descended*** to buddhahood". This line refers to the buddhas of the future who have not yet gained buddhahood. In this good aeon they are the nine hundred and ninety-eight future buddhas, starting with guardian Maitreya, who have not yet descended and, as well as that, the persons who are at present training in the conduct of enlightenment who in the future will definitely achieve buddhahood and who are equal in number to the stars in the sky and the grains of seed on the earth. If those future buddhas are prayed to and urged not to delay for a long time but to become buddhas ***most quickly*** or with the utmost speed, then they will ***complete*** all of what they have asserted they will do, their ***intentions***, so this is a method for causing them to gain the rank of complete ***enlightenment***. Having traversed in ***stages*** all the good qualities of the levels and paths, they must ***descend to buddhahood!***[61] Note that "descend" is in the imperative. In short, the meaning is "may all buddhas of the future quickly become buddhas!"

The reason for calling this "a prayer to wholly fulfill the intent" is that it is prayer for the quick accomplishment of what the future buddhas are now planning or intending to do.

2.1.1.3. Prayer to purify a buddha-field

> May the fields which exist in the ten directions,
> However many they are, be vast and wholly pure.
> May they be utterly filled with conquerors gone
> Before the leading bodhi tree and with buddha sons.

---

[61] The correct wording for this line is shown in the verse above. A mistaken tradition of explanation of the words appeared in Tibet several or more centuries ago. The mistaken explanation, which is now universal amongst Tibetans, is seen in this sentence. This wording and with it a mistaken explanation appears in three places in the prayer. The line is fully explained in Nāgārjuna's and my own commentary in volume I.

According to some commentaries, "*the fields which exist in the ten directions*" contains old terminology[62] and should be understood to mean "the fields—this one and that one and the other one—of the world realms of the ten directions". Some other commentaries say that this should be understood to mean "the fields situated in which places in the ten directions". Either way, may it be that the container worlds, **however many** of them that there are, do not have the ordinary rocks, stones, sharp objects, jagged mountains, and bumpy ground that are the features of impurity. Instead, may they be completely pure, being wide and lovely to behold throughout their extent as in the example of the Sukhāvatī field. Thus, may **they be vast and wholly pure** throughout their extent.

Not only the container world but the beings contained in it are to be pure. That means that there would not be a single sentient being of the ordinary type present whose mind is filled with affliction. Thus both container and contents are pure and because of that it is referred to with the words "for the purification of a field".

In the middle of that sort of place where both container and contents are pure, the nirmāṇakāyas of the buddhas at the time of becoming buddhas must sit with their backs to the bodhi tree then become buddhas. Therefore, having gone before the leading tree amongst trees, the excellent bodhi tree, they first, on the path of meditation, enter the equipoise of the Vajra-Like Samādhi then become conquerors over the army of regiments of the māras. For example, at the time of our teacher Śhākyamuni becoming buddha, he sat with the bodhi tree to his back then entered equipoise, then in the first watch of the night[63] subdued the māras, then in the midnight watch stayed in equipoise, then in the first part of the early

---

[62] The old terminology referred to here is the Tibetan term "ga la", which actually has the sense "wherever they could exist", and has been translated here as "which exist".

[63] ... the period from 8pm to 12pm.

morning, at the time of beating the drum of conquering, became a manifest buddha. Similarly, the buddhas of the ten directions in becoming buddhas also, having purified a field, sat with their backs to the bodhi tree, entered equipoise, defeated the māra regiments without exception, then became buddhas. **May** all the world realms **be utterly filled with conquerors** who have **gone before the leading** tree, the **bodhi tree, and with** their mind sons, the bodhisatva sons who have the three features, the **buddha sons**.

This part is a buddha's purification of a field. It is "the outer purification of a field". According to mantra, "purification of a field" refers to the time of realizing appearance and becoming as the universal purity; at that time, there is the realization of appearance and becoming as the maṇḍala of the three kāyas without the slightest presence of the atoms of the impure side. However we are following sutra here, so this concerns the purification of a field referred to in "threefold completion, ripening, and purifying"—it is a prayer for making container and contents of purity which is called "a prayer for purifying a field".

2.1.1.4. Prayer to benefit sentient beings

> May the sentient beings of the ten directions,
> However many, always be free of sickness and have ease.
> May all migrators' objectives of dharma be with
> Harmony and their hopes also be accomplished.

May the sentient beings of the ten directions—the sentient beings of the six classes of migrators who are as unending as the limits of space are unending, ***however many*** there are, ***always***, from today on for as long as they have not gained the rank of a buddha, because of my arousing the mind of the excellent thought for supreme enlightenment, engaging in the conduct of accumulating accumulations and purifying the obscurations, and creating connections through completely pure prayers, ***be free of sickness*** if they have the suffering of the karmic appearance of sickness, ***and*** have the ***ease***, within a state of not being separated from the dharma, of not the tiniest sensation of suffering arising in body, speech, or mind.

May it be that, **all migrators'** minds once they have been turned to the holy dharma and are seeking the **objectives of dharma**—threefold hearing, contemplating, meditating, and so on—**be with harmony**. In other words, may the migrators who seek dharma because they consider it to be meaningful be without the disharmony of mind of: falling into the biasses of tenets or being in disagreement over the vehicles higher and lower; or disagreeing with virtuous spiritual friends; or becoming lost in the conceit of learning and pride in general; or being jealous of others, condescending towards them, cursing them, and the like; or any other such disharmonies of mind. Instead, may faith, pure outlook, loving kindness and compassion, and the enlightenment mind be born in their mindstreams and then, viewing the companions of similarly pure conduct with whom they practise dharma as though both were born from the same parents, may they have the harmony of same thought and conduct when practising the holy dharma. *And*, based on that, no matter which of the conducts of the conqueror's sons—generosity, and so on—that any of the migrator sentient beings who seek dharma because it is meaningful wish to train in, may **their** mental **hopes also be** easily **accomplished**.

2.1.2. Prayer for not forgetting enlightenment mind

This has seven parts:

1. prayer for remembering the succession of lives
2. prayer for being ordained
3. prayer for pure discipline
4. prayer to be able to teach dharma in various languages
5. prayer for making effort at virtue
6. prayer not to forget enlightenment mind
7. prayer to be free from adverse circumstances

2.1.2.1. Prayer for remembering the succession of lives

> While I perform the conducts of enlightenment
> May I remember my births in all migrations.

This is praying that "In all of my lifetimes may I not be separated from the excellent thought of the enlightenment mind and **perform** and accomplish the excellent conduct of the ocean-like **conducts of** the conqueror's sons, the bodhisatvas or **enlightenment** heroes. I will need to go through many lifetimes yet **while** doing that, so may **I remember** the **births** I have taken on every occasion in my past succession of lives, what each one was **in all** the places good and bad of the six classes of **migrators**".

These two lines are a prayer to remember your succession of lives. If you remember a birth in which you truly practised dharma, it has great benefit for your practise of dharma now. Śhāntideva said:

> Until the level of Utter Joy has been gained,
> Always remembering my succession of lives ...[64]

If you remember your succession of lives, you will, knowing each of the non-virtuous evil karmas accumulated in those previous births, think of their result, the suffering to be experienced in the abodes of the bad migrations, and that in turn will allow you to sever the continuity of prior karmic debts and develop a frame of mind that avoids them. As well as that, you will, knowing each of the virtuous karmas you have accumulated in previous births, think of their result, the happiness to be experienced in the abodes of a higher levels, and that in turn will allow you to continue in the present with virtuous karmas. Remembering your succession of lives will also mean that you will have the determination and ability needed to withstand any hardships that have to be undergone in the pursuit of virtue. For example, at an earlier time when our teacher had taken

---

[64] Utter Joy is the first of the bodhisatva levels.

birth in the hell abode as the champion Pakṣhita, the force of compassion that came from caring about one person, his friend Kamarupa, caused him to be born in the Heaven of the Thirty Three. If there is that kind of benefit to compassion for a single sentient being, what need is there to state the benefit that there will be with having compassion that considers all sentient beings? Based on remembering births like this, your continuing on with that sort of compassion will enable you to give rise to compassion which considers all sentient beings.

Generally speaking, not only does the force of prayer bring the possibility of remembering births, but the force of meditation also brings the same possibility. Previously, when Patrul Rinpoche was staying in Vairochana's cave in the region Gyalmo Tsawa Rong, around midnight he asked the person sitting before him, "Do you remember your previous births?" The other offered, "I don't remember any at all." He said, "I remember many of my births. Previously in the Noble Land when I had a birth as a prostitute, the highly accomplished Kalacharya came along. I met him and, because of developing faith in him, removed all the jewellery from my body and offered it to him. He then made dedications and prayers, after which he said, that I would henceforth not need to take a birth as a woman."

Similarly, the learned and accomplished Rāga Asye has said that he remembered past births in a state of samādhi. Previously, Śhākyamuni Buddha had come and was turning the wheel of dharma in India, at which time he remembered having taken birth as a white dog. He told this to his disciples and explained that a band of robbers had a piece of meat which the dog stole so they caught the dog, bound its legs with rope, then threw it into a deep pit. At some point in time, a bhikṣhu who was a great holder of the Vinaya came along, made a prayer that the dog's bonds be undone, then departed. If you look now, that bhikṣhu is present as Śhāripūtra. Henceforth he will not need to take a dog's birth, the Buddha said.

If like that you remember your births, you will be able to sever the continuity of bad latencies, therefore, this is a prayer to remember your births. That being so, Jigmey Tennyi[65] was heard to say:

> It will be good if you recite this *Excellent Conduct Prayer* assiduously, but be careful while reciting it because what the words are saying might actually happen and you could remember, couldn't you?! The words are not the main thing, what they point at is the main thing.

Similarly, if you do not keep your mind on the meaning of the words, then as Patrul Rinpoche said:

> If you recite in an indeterminate way, you will not plant so much as a seed of emancipation!

Following on from his words, Khenpo Lungtog's camp has the saying, "Think, 'Did I plant even a seed of emancipation?' " So, if you recite this *Excellent Conduct* one time while carefully thinking of its meaning, it is certain that there will be many aeon's worth of gathering accumulations and cleansing obscurations with it; as Jigmey Tennyi said, "Even if all of the buddhas of the three times were to gather in one spot and confer they would not find a special kind of prayer better than this".

2.1.2.2. Prayer for being ordained [66]

> At death transfers and births in all successive lives
> May I always become ordained.

From today onwards for as long as I and others have not become buddhas, when for the sake of others I am training in the conduct of the conqueror's sons, may I *in all* of my births one after another, the whole *successive* string of *lives* one after another, not have the sort

---

[65] ... the third Dodrupchen ...

[66] For a full explanation of this verse and the issues around how it should be understand by Westerners, see my own commentary.

of mind that thinks of my own desires to enter a zone of cessation through severing the stream of births for my own sake as is done by the śhrāvakas and pratyekas of the Lesser Vehicle. Instead, through the force of having produced enlightenment mind in my mindstream, may I for the sake of all migrator sentient beings deliberately go through *"deaths, transfers, and births"*—death in the current life, followed by the transfer of going through the intervening state, followed by birth in the next life. To go through deaths, transfers, and births and all that goes with them entails taking countless births for the sake of migrators, but in order to be able to undertake that task without fear and small-minded rejection of it and also in order always to keep completely pure discipline until in those lives the levels have been attained, *may I* not take an ordinary householder's birth but *always become ordained*!

What is the meaning of bodhisatvas praying that, for as long as they have not attained the noble one's levels, they will gain the body of someone who is ordained? If they become householders, they have to protect their kin and end up using their time in the desire, anger, and stupidity of the eight worldly dharmas; they spend all their time on this life with the result that seeking what is meaningful is left behind and put off till a later life. For them, becoming a householder ends up being an obstacle to accomplishing holy dharma and enlightenment. It is like what conquerors' son Śhāntideva said:

> Until the level Utter Joy is gained
> May I become ordained.

After that first bodhisatva level has been attained, the bodhisatva is a person with mastery. Thus, no matter which birth is taken, it will be only for the others' sakes, so even though the body of a householder is taken, that bodhisatva will be one who has all good qualities and is free of stains. For that sort of person it is impossible for any behaviour not to turn into an assistant of bodhisatva conduct.

2.1.2.3. Prayer for pure discipline

> May I train following all the conquerors,
> Working to wholly complete the excellent conduct
> And doing the stainless, totally pure discipline conduct
> In a way that is always uncorrupted and faultless.

The basis is set with completely pure discipline then the motivating force is enlightenment mind. ***May I train following all the conquerors*** means to have the excellent motivation of seeking to benefit others not mixed with the bad mind that thinks of your own wants. At the time of training following all the conquerors, the conquerors' sons', the bodhisatvas' ***excellent*** thought consisting of both fictional and superfactual enlightenment minds is to be aroused and their excellent ***conduct*** of the four things of gathering, the six pāramitās, and so on is to be ***worked*** at in order ***to wholly complete*** it.

And, within the training in excellent conduct, training in the higher training of discipline is especially important because it is the basis for all good qualities—as has been said:

> Discipline, like the ground of movement and non-
>   movement,
> Is the basis for all good qualities, it was nicely taught.[67]

This ***discipline*** type of ***conduct*** motivated by enlightenment mind is referred to as being "stainless, thoroughly pure" because it is ***without stains*** of the afflictions and ***totally pure*** given that it is not cloaked by the thought of finding a place of personal peace—like that of the Lesser Vehicle shrāvakas and pratyekabuddhas—meaningful. May I be able to engage in this precious discipline ***in a way that is always uncorrupted***, like a lotus flower, uncloaked by the bad actions of lax discipline! ***And*** it also says ***"faultless"*** which means to

---

[67] The ground of this earth allows for all movement and non-movement of the beings on it and likewise discipline is a basis for all good qualities, it was nicely taught by the Buddha.

keep it without the stains of clinging to truth in the three spheres[68] and without the faults of those things in your mindstream which would be inimical to keeping good discipline. Note that, if you are proud of your own keeping of discipline and disparage others over their loose discipline, it is much worse than having loose discipline yourself. In regard to this, previously, two great geshes fell into disharmony when one geshe, having heard of loose discipline in the other, happily disparaged the other, and the other, when he heard those disparaging words to the effect that he had abandoned his discipline, showed anger. Among the two, whose bad behaviour was greater?

That being so, *Maitreya's Prayer* says:

> With rules of discipline free of fault and
> Discipline which has complete purity,
> May I, through discipline without conceit
> Complete the discipline pāramitā.

The "conceit" there is thinking to yourself that you are staying within the rules then with pride disparaging others whose discipline is corrupt. That being so, may I, from today on for as long as I have not reached the heart of enlightenment, always do the completely pure discipline in a way which is uncorrupted, faultless.

2.1.2.4. Prayer to be able to teach dharma in various languages

> I will teach dharma in all languages—
> In gods, nāgas, and yakṣhas' languages,
> In khumbandha and mens' languages and
> In all migrators' languages many as there are.

The buddhas teach dharma in a miraculous fashion like this:

> One instance of speech appears as one hundred instances of speech ...

---

[68] The three spheres in any action are the agent, object, and action.

and like this:

> Like this: the questions of all sentient beings
> Petitioned by them all at once
> Are answered with but one intonation of speech.[69]

When we have gained all the good qualities of the bodhisatvas, we will know various languages. Accordingly, this prayer is made now to create the dependent connection needed to be able one day to have a buddha's kind of speech so as to be able to ripen those to be tamed by being able to teach dharma in various languages.

I will teach dharma in gods, nāgas, and yakṣhas' languages and *in Khumbandha*—a type of humanoid with a body like a vase and very sweet sounding speech that ravishes away the listener's mind—language. *And* I will teach dharma in the countless *mens' languages*—Indian language which alone has three hundred and sixty different types, and Tibetan, Mongolian, and so on languages. *And* I will teach dharma *in all* the six types of *migrators'* various countless *languages* as *many as there are* and which have just been illustrated by the ones mentioned above. Moreover, each migrator will be able to understand what I say in his own language. For example, if a phrase like "all compounds are impermanent" is expressed just once, each migrator will be able to understand it in his own language no matter which of all the different languages it is. Moreover, each migrator will be able to understand what I say in accordance with his own level of understanding within the vehicles. In that way, through generosity of dharma which has nothing out of place in it, I will teach dharma. Note that the words "will teach dharma" actually are in the past tense "have taught the dharma", but

---

[69] The actual words are from a sutra:
> It is like this: if all sentient beings asked
> Many ascertaining questions all at once,
> In one moment of mind it would be taken in,
> Then a single intonation of speech would give reply to each one, and in each one's own language.

in his commentary Patrul says that it must be understood as a prayer saying "may I be able to teach dharma".[70]

2.1.2.5. Prayer for making effort at virtue

Gentled, I'll be most diligent at the pāramitās;

Here **"*gentled*"** is a term meaning having a mind with good disposition, one that is tamed and peaceful. Someone who is training in the conduct of enlightenment but who does not have his three doors tamed and pacified, is not going about it the right way. Although the family of the Great Vehicle has many good qualities, the primary one was taught to be that one's mindstream should be gentled mainly through kindness and love. Thus, the three doors should be pacified and tamed, like gruel soup with butter added or wool whose lumps have been pressed out with a smoothing tool[71]. Whoever you are with, your behaviour should be gentle, making you pleasant to be around, like a belt for the waist, and you must with great loving kindness engage in the enlightenment conduct of the six pāramitās, and so on. The conquerors' sons' conduct is vast as an ocean and difficult to do but you must be ***most diligent at the*** practise of the ***pāramitās***, taking joy in the practise, like geese coming down to a lake adorned with lotuses or children entering a grove of flowers and fruit trees or elephants oppressed by heat entering a pool of water

---

[70] This is correct. There are many places in the prayer where the verse does not have the words "may I" but ends in the future tense of the relevant verb. In Sanskrit, this was a way of indicating an aspiration and intent to complete that aspiration. It is the same as announcing in English "I shall do it!"

[71] The addition of butter makes what is otherwise a very coarse and rough food smooth and pleasant. Woolen carpets just off the loom have many hard lumps in them, so the whole carpet is gone over with a special tool that removes them, making the otherwise rough carpet very smooth.

without hesitation. This single line presents the making of a prayer for diligently working at virtue.

2.1.2.6. Prayer not to forget enlightenment mind

    I will never forget enlightenment mind.

This set of five things above—remembering successive lives, being ordained, having pure discipline, teaching dharma through various languages, and persevering at virtue—are sub-topics of the main topic of not forgetting enlightenment mind. Thus, this line now says, "in all of my births one after another, the whole string of successions of lives one after another, may it be that *I will never*, not so much as for even a moment, *forget* the two types of precious *enlightenment mind*".

This precious enlightenment mind is all the conqueror's eighty-four thousand dharma doors distilled down to a single essence. If you have it, all other instructions give way to it. It is one medicine able to cure one hundred illnesses, like a universal panacea. It is without mistake the seed that is the actual cause for accomplishing buddhahood. All other means for gathering accumulations and cleansing obscurations were shown as methods for producing this precious enlightenment mind in the mindstream.

Previously there was Jowo Je Dīpaṃkāra, who was the sugata Amitābha in fact. He had gone to Bodhgaya to do circumambulations where he was thinking about what the primary dharma for gaining buddhahood in one life should be. One time while circumambulating, he came across two clay statues conferring with each other. One said to the other, "What is the primary dharma for gaining buddhahood in one life?" The other said, "If one needs to obtain buddhahood in one life, the precious enlightenment mind is the primary one."

Similarly, the great Kadampa Putowa said:

> From the time I was small until now, except for thinking only of the sake of other sentient beings, I have not had a thought for so much as a moment of my own sake.

That is the sort of thing we need. So, from today until we one day gain the rank of a buddha, it is important to make prayers not to be separated from the precious mind of enlightenment.

The Buddha Bhagavat said:

> I will separate from the body but may I not separate from the mind!

Because of karma everyone without exception, even the smallest creatures like ants, will separate from the body but will not separate from the mind, so we need to pray again and again not to be separated from the enlightenment mind. If we separate from that mind and join with the karmas of evil deeds, then, even if we had the body of a great king able to wield power over a whole world realm and were of high family with beautiful youthful form, strength, and sovereign power, and were someone put above everyone's crown, we would during countless births fall lower and lower within the abodes of bad migrations. Struck by unbearable suffering—duḥkha—there would be no opportunity for emancipation. If we remain unseparated from it, then, even if we do not get anything more than a weak and ineffective body and do not have the physical ability to work to benefit others now, because of having the mind that seeks to benefit others, we still have entered something with the same sort of meaning. The *Commentary on the Meaning of Enlightenment Mind* says:

> Though without the power to do the work of benefiting others,
> Anyone for whom that mind has become present
> Has entered its meaning.

The Sutra of Giving Advice to the King says:

> The buddha bhagavat said, "Great King, you have many works and purposes so cannot accomplish them all, but

never forget this compassion which considers sentient beings! Furthermore, you shall not train in the many dharmas of those who desire the rank of a buddha, you shall train in one dharma. If you ask what that single one is, it is great compassion."

Great compassion is like a seed which is the uncommon actual cause of giving birth to the precious mind of enlightenment in your own mindstream. All other gathering accumulations and cleansing obscurations is like water, manure, and warmth, the conditions for getting the sprout of enlightenment mind to grow. If a true form of this great compassion has been produced in the mindstream, it is as though all of the buddha dharmas are sitting in the palm of your hand.

If the precious enlightenment mind is present in the mindstream, even if you are born in the birthplaces of the animals, it will be like previously, when the Buddha Bhagavat was on the path of training and deliberately took birth as a tortoise.

This part of the prayer is saying, "In dependence on the above five types of causes, may I never forget this precious enlightenment mind!"

2.1.2.7. Prayer to be free from adverse circumstances

> May the evils become obscurations
> Without exception be wholly cleansed.

If you want to produce the precious enlightenment mind in your mindstream, you will need to free yourself of the factors that could become adverse to it. If you do not, they can come into effect and then, because they are non-virtuous evils, they will be the cause of unpleasant karmic ripenings. They can be motivated by any of the three poisons, so it is possible for them to cause all of the different types of accumulation of non-virtuous evil but, in short, ***may the evils*** all of which have ***become obscurations*** to the precious enlightenment mind, and their seeds and latencies too, in their entirety—*without exception*—*be wholly cleansed* by the forces of the outstanding antidote to evil, the enlightenment mind, the view which realizes emptiness, and so on.

2.1.3. Prayer for which is uncloaked or undefiled

> May I be free of karma, affliction, and māra's works,
> And though as migrators of the world, have conduct
> Which is like the way a lotus is unaffected by water,
> And like the sun and moon are unhindered in the sky.

"Karma" here refers to the bad karmas of the ten non-virtues, five immediate ones, four heavy ones, eight wrong ones, and so on[72]. "Affliction" refers to the five root afflictions, the twenty proximate afflictions, and so on. For "māra's works" it has been said, "If you are a person who exerts himself from the heart with intense exertion at the holy dharma, the path of enlightenment, the more profound the dharma, the greater the māras" and "those who have perseverance in their practice will have more hostility from māras". Now if you are not freed from the hostile ones who bring many obstacles physical and mental—the māras, gyalgong dre, senmo tsan, the'u rang[73], and so on—you will not accomplish the sake of others as it should be done, therefore, it is necessary to pray to "to be free of all obstacles like the sun is free of clouds", which is done here with "*May I be free of karma, afflictions, and māra's works*". If you are a person who practises dharma from the depths of his heart, you will

---

[72] The first two are about specific actions that do not depend on a vow being broken. The next is the four defeats of a monk or nun. The next is breakage of a set of eight vows.

[73] Māras are four specific forces or events that block one's spiritual progress completely. Gyalgong dre are a male type of malevolent spirit and senmo tsan a seductive female one; they are also personifications of unhealthy mental states that steal a practitioner away from dharma practice. The'u rang are small gnomes who live on others' energy.

investigate "In what I am doing, will the māras easily find an opportunity to create many obstacles?" If you are otherwise—someone who does not practise dharma—the māras have no need to make any obstacles for you because you have already fall under the control of obstacles.

Generally speaking, even if you have not previously accumulated a bad karmic cause from which obstacles can arise, it is possible suddenly to fall under the control of māra's obstacles. Therefore, if you supplicate the guru and Three Jewels, develop trust in karma and its results, and make good prayers again and again, you will not fall under the control of māra's obstacles. Gemang Onpo Tenga said:

> Make supplications to the guru Orgyan Lord and
> There will be no falling under the control of the
>   circumstances for obstacles to arise.

Thus it is necessary to supplicate the Orgyan Lord[74] and the Three Jewels. If we do not, no matter who of us it is, from the first it will be as though we enjoy having something happen that we do not want to happen. Even if we are sure that we do not want bad things to happen, once we fall under the control of māra's obstacles, samsara's bad things will be there circling over our heads out of our control, therefore we must be careful! It is like the young monks who have entered the dharma path know that if they look up from their studies, an older disciplinary monk could easily appear over them, so they stay in their seats keeping good behaviour. However, one day when māra's obstacle enters the heart of one of them, that one will have a bad thought which will lead him to do something bad and then after that all of his inner thoughts will definitely be problematic.

It is necessary, as explained above, to be freed from the works of māra that come from karma and afflictions. It is also necessary for

---

[74] ... Padmasambhava ...

the sake of other sentient beings to go, in rebirth over and again, into the worlds, meaning the abodes of the six classes of migrators. ***Though*** you seem to be the same ***as*** the other ***migrators of* those worlds**, you ***have conduct*** that is different from theirs. You enter those abodes whilst maintaining the conduct of a bodhisatva. Thus you are in the samsaric abodes as someone who, by the power of enlightenment mind and realizing emptiness, is not cloaked by any karmas and afflictions arising through doing things for his own sake. You have conduct ***which is like the way a lotus*** growing up from a swamp is ***unaffected*** or unharmed ***by*** the swampy ***water***. You stay in samsara but, because you are not cloaked with the faults of samsara, everything you do becomes done only for the sake of other sentient beings. Even if you adhere to the behaviour of an untouchable libidinous woman or butcher or prostitute, it can only become deeds done only for the sake of other sentient beings. In this regard, Jigmey Lingpa said:

> Kingly caste, lordly caste, common caste, brahman caste,
> Outcaste, woman, fine youth, spiritual seeker ...[75]

While doing deeds for the sake of other sentient beings there is a need to be able to remain unharmed and unstopped by any obstacle, so it says, "***And*** may I be able to conduct myself for the sake of migrators without hindrance, ***like the sun and moon*** move ***unhindered in the sky***. Some commentaries explain it this way:

> If causes and conditions are complete, the dawning of the sun will be stopped and the trees in the fields will not be able to push their heads up past the stones in the ground, so this is a prayer for having the ability to work for

---

[75] The first four are the four castes of Indian Hindu society; they include everyone in the land. The remainder are all sorts of people who usually would not be considered as suited to dharma practice but who, from a higher perspective, can be considered as such.

migrators' sake like the sun shining and ripening the vegetation.

Other styles of commentarial explanation are:

Like clouds, darkness, haze, and so on do not harm the sun, may I not be cloaked in any fault that would prevent finalization of the two sakes and be able to conduct myself for others' benefit without retributions or unwanted circumstances.

And:

When the sun and moon move without hindrance through the heavens, they assist by ripening vegetation and harvests and do so without conceived efforts, and like that, when bodhisatvas work to work to bring benefit and ease to all sentient beings may they be able to work for migrators' sakes without retributions or unwanted circumstances.

Although there are these various ways of commenting on this verse, I do not think there is any contradiction.[76]

2.1.4. Prayer to set sentient beings in benefit and ease

For as much as the area of a field and directions
I'll utterly pacify the suffering of the bad migrations
Then set all migrators in the best of happinesses;
I will perform conduct that benefits all migrators.

The first line is saying "**For as much as** is **the area**, height, width, **directions**, and so on of a **field** of the pure side, a buddha-*field* ..." How much that is cannot be fathomed by the mind of an ordinary being no matter how hard he tries because it is outside the reach of his type of mind. For the impure fields too, the area of the

---

[76] Again, there are many ways of explaining this verse found even in the Indian commentaries. The simplest way is what he says first and that fits with Nāgārjuna's commentary to this verse.

containers and number of sentient beings contained in them are likewise not measurable. Thus, there is no need to mention that the number of migrators existing in the ***bad migrations*** in the hell, preta, animal, and so on abodes also is not fathomable by that type of mind. So, in reliance on the forces of the blessings of the pure fields, the compassionate activity of the buddhas seated in them, and my prayers coming from the completely pure special intention, and so on, may it be possible for ***the suffering*** without exception ***of*** all sentient beings in ***the*** three ***bad migrations***, and so on to be ***utterly pacified***. Here, Dzogchen Patrul's oral tradition says that you should radiate unfathomable amounts of light rays from your body, which, when they hit all sentient beings of the six classes—the hells, and so on—free them from the latencies of the sufferings that are the individual karmic appearances of the six classes and that you should then make that prayer again and again.

Like that, the power that comes from the compassionate activity of the Three Jewels, the force of the truth of dharmatā, and your own prayers made with the completely pure special intention, empties the abodes of the three bad migrations. Following that, there is a prayer "May I ***then***, in a temporary way, ***set all migrators*** of the three bad migrations ***in the best of happinesses*** of the good existences of the higher levels. And not only that but ultimately for all migrators, may I by teaching them the path of the three vehicles satisfy them with the holy dharma as they pass through a string of happy existences in the higher levels. In other words, may it be that ***I will perform conduct*** of the sort ***that*** temporarily ***benefits all migrators*** and ultimately sets them at the level of unsurpassed complete buddhahood.

2.1.5. Prayer for wearing armour

> I will work at completing enlightenment conduct,
> Enter in harmony with sentient beings' conduct,
> And utterly teach the excellent conducts;
> May I do this throughout all future aeons.

"Wearing the armour of courage" refers to rousing courage rather than cowering in the face of having to perform one of the difficult-to-do conducts of enlightenment, then declaring that you will do it. So, you create the armour of courage which thinks, "I alone accept the burden of setting all sentient beings pervading the limits of space at the rank of an unsurpassable complete buddha". Then, in order to ripen yourself, you think, "Now, I arouse the thought for it, the mind of supreme enlightenment. For the actual conduct, the six pāramitās which are the practices of the conquerors' sons include even having to perform the generosity of giving head and limbs, but for as long as I have not completed them, I will fully armour myself with the armour of courage that is willing to make intense efforts". Thus it says, "*I will work at completing enlightenment conduct*".

And then, in order to ripen others, you think, "Not contaminated by the bad mind which thinks of my own sake and in order to be involved only with the sakes of others, I will gradually lead the mind that shows hostility to those who are angry and attachment to those who have desire to dharma. In doing so, I will engage them with conduct that they find agreeable. Thus it says, "*I will enter in harmony with sentient beings' conduct*". With that you are making the prayer, "May I be able to armour myself with the armour of that sort of courage". Previously, Buddha Śhākyamuni kept to this approach of conduct in accordance with the ways of the world by entering a womb, surrounding himself with a retinue of queens, and so on.

And, motivated by the excellent thought of enlightenment mind and engaging in the six pāramitās which are the excellent conducts of the conquerors' sons, I will *utterly teach* them—meaning teach them to the utmost of my ability—*the excellent conducts*. For that, I will teach them all of the instructions on the modes of training in the bodhisatva's trainings with none kept hidden or secret.

Then, having armoured myself with those three ways of wearing the armour of courage to set all sentient beings on the level of great enlightenment—completion, entering, and having entered—*may I do this throughout all future aeons*, that is, for as long as it would take to reach the limits of space, and do so without weariness.

Many observations have been made at this point by Tibetan experts about enlightenment conduct and excellent conduct, each one being an explanation that attempts to fit with what has been said in this verse, but they do not agree. Other experts say, "To explain this verse, it has to be recognized that it has been written in the style of the sutras of the noble land".

2.1.6. Prayer to have the company of companions of the same lot

> May I always be accompanied by those
> Whose conduct matches my own!
> Moreover, through body, speech, and mind
> I will perform the same conducts and prayer.

This is a prayer that in all successive lives, at the time of training in the conducts of the conquerors, you will not be apart from companions whose view and conduct are in harmony with your own. Dromtonpa was heard to say:

> Until one has gained the levels, it is necessary to arrange
> to have virtuous companions and avoidance of death.

He meant that until you have gained the levels, you need to have virtuous companions and also need to avoid death, that is, to stay alive. After gaining the levels, you cannot be misled by companions who engage in evil, but until then, you need the company of excellent companions, ones who are like medicinal trees, so it is necessary to pray: "May the conduct of my three doors be in harmony with or fitting with that of virtuous companions".

When doing my training in enlightenment conduct, I am to exert myself at the practise of Samantabhadra's conduct, the six pāramitās of conquerors' sons' conduct, so *may I always* have the company of *those* excellent dharma companions, medicinal trees *whose conduct* is of a sort that **matches** that of **my own** view and conduct. And, having their company may it be, **moreover,** that **I will through body, speech, and mind perform conducts and prayer** that are of **the same** sort and style, a match with theirs.

The second couplet has the following meaning. Having the company of dharma companions who are medicinal trees, may I have harmony of view and conduct in regard to the bodily conducts of performing generosity, and so on, and of keeping the disciplines such as providing protection for sentient beings who fear for their lives, and so on. And may I have harmony of view and conduct in respect to the spoken conducts of speaking the truth, reconciling those with grudges, speaking nicely, telling stories to help others tame themselves, and so on. And may I have harmony of view and conduct in respect to the mental conducts of having an attitude of giving, an attitude of benefiting, a content mind with little desire, trust in the profound view of karma and result, and, in short, in thoughts only of benefiting other. And may there also be harmony in respect to making prayers: like Buddha Śhākyamuni who previously made five hundred great prayers when he was on the path of training and like guardian Amitābha who also made five hundred great prayers when he was on the path of training in his life as the bhikṣhu Chokyi Jungnay, may I too train following those buddhas, making prayers of aspiration through having thoughts and actions the same as companions whose view and conduct are in harmony with mine.

To give an example, companions with harmonious view and conduct are like Maudgyalyāyana and Śhāriputra who were, within the large retinue of the Buddha Bhagavat, the ones best at miracles and prajñā respectively. The force of their previously-made prayers meant that from the time they were young, nothing either one heard could separate them. And, the two of them heard dharma and did three-fold hearing, contemplation, and meditation together in front of Buddha. And, in terms of path, they explained together the four baskets of the authoritative statements[77] showing the practice of the three trainings. And, in terms of fruition, they obtained the same rank of arhat.

2.1.7. Prayer to attend to and please a virtuous spiritual friend

> Companions who wish to benefit me,
> The ones who utterly teach excellent conduct—
> May I always be with them!
> I will never displease them!

The **companions** who are gurus or spiritual friends **who wish to benefit me** and spiritual friends who keep me away from lesser or wrong paths are excellent companions who teach me the path of emancipation correctly then travel the enlightenment path together with me, so they are described here as "companions". Companions or spiritual friends of that sort are **the ones who utterly teach** or fully explain to me this wish-fulfilling jewel of a prayer called "***Excellent Conduct***"[78] that is concerned with the specially noble path for accomplishing enlightenment, teaching it to me through their minds of great loving kindness in order to ripen and liberate my mindstream. **May I** throughout the strings of successions of my lives one after another **always be with them**, those spiritual friends who will do that for me. After meeting with holy spiritual friends of that sort, there is the question of how to attend them? **I will never** do bad actions of my three doors that would ***displease*** or upset their minds—that would upset them, that they would find unacceptable,

---

[77] Skt. agama. This is one of the twelve sections of the sutras.

[78] This commentary says that the words "excellent conduct" in this verse mean this prayer of Samantabhadra. However, Indian sources and Yeshe De say that these words do not represent the proper name of Samantabhadra's prayer but the name of excellent conduct in general. You will note that the actual words of the verse are "who teach excellent conduct (in general)" not "who teach the excellent conduct (prayer of Samantabhadra).

that would make them turn away, and so on. Instead, through engaging in the three ways of pleasing them, may I be able to supplicate at their feet, accomplish what they have in mind, remain in harmony with their thought and actions, and especially be able to accept their understanding, and in that way, may I be able to serve ***them***.

2.1.8.1. Prayer for making the tathagatas visible

> I will always view the conquerors in direct perception,
> The guardians, buddhas surrounded by their sons.

May ***I always view*** the countenances of ***the conquerors***, the faces on their nice form bodies with the marks and signs clear and complete, seeing them with my eyes ***in direct perception***. "Always view" their faces does not mean that one will view them and then again later on view them but that one will continuously view them because of being, as Lochen Rinpoche[79] said, "a conqueror of the non-virtuous dharmas" and then viewing them from that time on. ***The*** conquerors are also known as ***guardians*** because they stand by and protect migrator sentient beings. They are the ***buddhas*** seated in the fields in the boundless, limitless universes of the ten directions as well as the bodhisatvas whom they ***are surrounded by***, ***their*** unfathomable heart ***sons***. Thus, this is a prayer to view continuously, with one's own eyes, the faces of the buddhas or conquerors.

2.1.8.2. Having seen their faces, a prayer to make offerings

> I will also make vast offerings to them
> In all future aeons without wearying.

The buddhas of the three times and ten directions and the buddhas' heart sons, the bodhisatvas, are seated in unfathomable numbers, in numbers equal to the atoms of the world realms situated on the area

---

[79] This means Lochen Dharmashrī, whose commentary is the original source for this particular commentarial tradition.

of one atom. Within their view, I will manifest my body so that it is equal in number to the field atoms, then *I will* greatly please them by *also making vast offerings to them* of the various offerings explained earlier, such as the surpassed and unsurpassed offerings. And I will do that *in all future aeons without wearying* of it—without tiring of and rejecting it, or the like—but with a fresh[80], admiring, and joyful mind.

2.1.9. A prayer for wholly holding the holy dharma

> Holding the holy dharma of the conquerors
> And fully illuminating enlightenment conduct,
> I will completely purify the excellent conduct
> And moreover will do that in all future aeons.

This is a prayer as follows. "Using the power of non-forgetfulness, I will be *holding* with nothing left out all of *the holy dharma of the conquerors* however much they taught, their excellent speech equal to the limits of space consisting of the eighty-four thousand dharma doors which are the antidotes for the eighty-four thousand afflictions, and so on. *And* I will practise it using threefold hearing, contemplation, and meditation, and so gain realization and liberate my mind with it, manifesting for my own sake the rank of dharmakāya, and not only that but will, for aeon after aeon, be *illuminating for all*[81] other sentient beings these unending-as-an-ocean *enlightenment conducts* by utterly teaching it to them. By illuminating for them how the enlightenment conducts apply to their body, speech, and mind, their mindstreams will be ripened and liberated, then I will have enacted the compassionate activity of doing great benefit

---

[80] "Fresh" here means "not tired".

[81] The words on this line can be understood to mean "fully illuminate for sentient beings" or "illuminate for all sentient beings". The earlier commentaries all show that it means the former, because of a point of Sanskrit grammar, but this meaning has been lost in Tibetan and the other meaning has been taken up as seen in here in this commentary.

by liberating others' mind streams, which sets up the dependent connection for a nirmāṇakāya for others' sake. And, in the context of all sentient beings, myself and others, training with great exertion in supreme bodhisatva Samantabhadra's conduct, that is, in the thoroughly excellent, completely pure enlightenment conduct like that, *I will completely purify the excellent conduct.* Note: Lochen said that the term given as "purify" here can have either of two meanings: "to train up" as in "to improve" or "to clean" as in "to purify". Here it means "purify" in the sense of cleaning away everything that does not accord with it—the mass of karma and afflictions, the bad mind which thinks of my own sake, and so on, all of those things that obstruct enlightenment conduct. *And moreover will* without weariness *do that in all future aeons.*"

2.1.10. Prayer for acquiring an unending store

> May I in re-entering all becomings
> Acquire unending merits and wisdoms.
> May I become an unending store of method, prajñā,
> Samādhis, complete emancipations, and all good qualities.

Bodhisatvas need to take birth not through a thought like that of the śrāvakas and pratyekas but through the thought of others' sake, which is what it is referring to when he says ,"*May I in* deliberately *re-entering* or taking birth again and again all *all* the abodes of the *becomings* which make up the three realms with its six classes of migrators". The bodhisatvas who have not gained the levels have to re-enter samsara because of karma. The bodhisatvas who have gained the levels also have to re-enter samsara, though in their case they take birth as a variety of emanations due to the forces arising from their mastery of prayers and samādhi and they do that for the sake of migrators. At the time of having taken such a birth, may I gain mastery over or *obtain* a treasure that is like *an unending store* of the referenced accumulation of *merit* of generosity, discipline, patience, perseverance, and so on, which is the cause of accomplishing a buddha's form body in the future, *and* may I gain mastery over or acquire an unending store, an ocean-like accumulation, of reference-less ***wisdom***[82] through meditating on lack of self and emptiness, and so on, the cause of gaining the complete knowing of a buddha, which is the ultimate.

May I become an unending store of method … "Method" means that in one moment of conduct done with the skilful means of the bodhisatva, an accumulation of many aeons is completed, as with the accumulation of forty thousand aeons of merit that occurred when a ship's captain of the past killed, out of compassion, a bad man intending to use a knife to kill the other passengers. "***Prajñā***" is, for example, the threefold prajñā of hearing, contemplating, and meditating. It is also the prajñā of the fictional which knows good and bad, and what to accept and reject, and is the prajñā of the superfactual which realizes actuality, emptiness. In ***samādhi*** there are the Illusion-Like, Going as a Hero, Vajra-Like, and so on samādhis, the many hundreds of samādhis had by the great bodhisatvas. Generally speaking, the term "samādhi" in Sanskrit language is used to mean a "tranquil state of mind". There are many ways to explain "***complete emancipation***"—the eight complete emancipations, and so on—but Patrul Rinpoche said that it refers here to the ability of the complete emancipation produced in reliance on method and prajñā, for example, a samādhi which is able to transform an aeon into an instant and one which is able to transform an instant into an aeon. Based on the method, prajñā, samādhis, complete emancipations, and five extra-perceptions—the five eyes, and so on—a bodhisatva develops an unending store of ***all*** the infinite ***good qualities***.

In other words, this verse is saying, "Just as a king has a storehouse of treasures that contains an inexhaustible array of useful items, at the time I am going from life to life in samsara for the sake of others, the ones to be tamed, may it be that I develop for my use a store of

---

[82] Referencing is an operation of dualistic mind. Wisdom has no referencing.

the inconceivable good qualities—method, prajñā, samādhi, complete emancipations, and so on—which arise from wisdom".

2.1.11. Prayer for entering, having eight enterings
2.1.11.1. Entering viewing the fields and buddhas

> On one atom are fields as many as the atoms
> And in those fields inconceivable buddhas
> Seated at the centre of their buddha sons;
> Doing enlightenment conduct, I will view them.
>
> Like that so too in all directions without exception
> On the breadth of merely a hair there's an ocean of buddhas
> Many as their measure in the three times and an ocean of fields
> And for an ocean of aeons doing the conduct, I'll utterly enter them.

On top of *one atom*, fathomless buddha-*fields* equal in number to however *many atoms* of the world realms of the ten directions there are will be able to be seen without their being squeezed or cramped and without their interfering with or being mixed up with the others *and in those fields*—this one and that one—an *inconceivable* number of *buddhas* are seated there, their bodies with marks and signs obvious and complete, their speech clear with empty sounds and indestructible dharma, and their minds bright with luminous-empty wisdom. Such buddhas are, moreover, *seated at the centre of* their *buddha sons*—their mind *sons*, the bodhisatvas, who wholly surround them, where they are perpetually turning the wheel of dharma for them. This is a prayer, "May I too, together with those bodhisatvas surrounding them, see the buddhas' faces in direct perception, hear them speak and so listen to the dharma taught by them, hold all the meanings of their dharma words with non-forgetfulness, assist the ones connected with them to be tamed, and so on. In those ways, may it be that *I will* be able *to do* the ocean-like *enlighten-*

ment conducts and have the fortune of being able to *view them* with their bodies adorned with the marks and signs of a buddha."

Like that described there that there are, on top of a single atom, countless field realms and buddhas and bodhisatva sons, *so too in the directions of all*[83] areas of fields of those world realms *without exception* yet for example *on the breadth of merely* the tip of *a* single *hair there is an ocean of buddhas* as *many as the measure of* the buddhas who will have descended *in the three times*. "Ocean" throughout this verse conveys the sense of a countless number. And with the buddhas is an ocean of buddha sons, the bodhisatvas. *And*, likewise, there is *an ocean of field* realms. All of this being present in that way is the nature of how things are in reality. It is not possible for this to appear in the minds of us ordinary beings now, but the bodhisatvas seated on the high levels and the buddhas are able to have it appear to them like that. This becomes a prayer: "May it be that I too am able to stay for a long time, *an ocean of aeons*, in front of the buddhas who in that way are countless, see their faces and listen to their dharma, make offerings, gather the accumulations, and make ocean-like prayers for aeons as long as there are field atoms, in other words, *doing the conduct and utterly entering* inconceivable enlightenment conducts in *them*"[84].

That is entering into viewing the buddhas' faces and viewing the oceanic field realms.

---

[83] This explanation is mistaken due to misunderstanding Sanskrit syntax. The "all" and "without exception" go with "directions".

[84] This explanation is mistaken due to misunderstanding Sanskrit syntax. Indian commentaries point out that "utterly enter" refers to entering into viewing the buddhas in direct perception and that "doing the conduct" follows on from that and means to engage in the enlightenment conducts while actually being present with the buddhas.

2.1.11.2. Entering the buddha speech

> Through the ocean of branches of sound in one speech,
> The complete purity of the branches of voice of all conquerors,
> Coming as voices exactly in accord with all migrators' thoughts,
> The buddha speech, is what I will perpetually enter.

Though one buddha teaches with *one* instance of *speech*, it has the feature that countless various sounds of the *ocean*—where ocean means like the number of atoms in an ocean—*of* buddha *voice* can appear in the individual domains of fathomless migrators. *Through* that key point, the speech of *all* other *conquerors* as well is likewise unending, ocean-like, and has voices of speech—the sixty *branches of voice* and so on—that have the special feature of their *complete purity* that makes it possible for them to appear in the domains of sentient beings in accord with the various makeup, faculties, and thoughts of migrator sentient beings. Therefore, when the buddhas turn the wheel of dharma, their speech acts to teach *all migrators*—the gods, asuras, kinnaras, nāgas, yakṣhas, and so on—each one in its own language and in accordance with its makeup, faculties, and thoughts. For example, the beings to be tamed no matter to which vehicle of the nine vehicles they belong will be taught with speech having the *voices* of Brahmā *that exactly accords with* their specific *thoughts* and mental capacities. At that time, *I will* listen to all of what all the buddhas teach and hold it with non-forgetfulness, will contemplate its meaning, and will meditate on that meaning. Thus I will, through threefold hearing, contemplation, and meditation, *perpetually enter the speech of the buddhas*. Note that Lochen said, "'Perpetually enter the speech of the buddhas means 'I will understand the infinite speech of all the conquerors and will not enter into blocking and not engaging with even one of them' ".)

2.1.11.3. Entering into turning the dharma wheel

> All the conquerors gone in the three times'
> Utter turning of the modes of the wheel
> And also their unending voices of speech
> I too will, by the force of rational mind, utterly enter.

This is praying "May I be able to turn the dharma wheel". *All*—however many there are—*of the conquerors gone* or descended *in the three times* turn the dharma wheel for the infinite sentient beings to be tamed. They *utterly turn* it by turning various *modes of the* dharma *wheel*—the three stages of the dharma wheel, and so on—for the various makeup, faculties, and thoughts of each of the beings to be tamed. This way of utterly turning the wheel of dharma is the buddhas' way of turning the wheel. There is the prayer that "Now I too will arouse the mind of supreme enlightenment, train in the conduct of the conquerors' sons, accumulate an ocean of the two accumulations, then, at the time of becoming a manifest complete buddha, I also will have the speech with sixty intonations of voice. When I turn the dharma wheel for others, the ones to be tamed, based on *also* having the ability to use *their unending* dharma *voices of* the conquerors' speech, *I too will, by the force of rational mind* that comes with my wisdom mind knowing all superficies, *utterly enter* the buddhas' speech with its sixty intonations of Brahmā's voice".

The words of the verse before this "I will perpetually enter into the buddha's speech" mean "when the buddha speech with its sixty intonations of voice teaches dharma to those to be tamed, I will perpetually enter it through listening to and retaining it". This verse means "When I have become a buddha and turn the wheel of dharma for others, I will enter their inexhaustible speech by force of rational mind", so the meanings of the two are not the same. Changkya Rolpa'i Dorje says that the former is merely hearing the language of the speech of inconceivable voices whereas for this one there has to be sight of wisdom so that the different meanings of the turnings of the wheel of dharma are not mixed up. He says that there is great difference here, which is the difference between the good qualities of the lower and higher levels, and that is how this has to be understood. The realized understanding of the minds behind their two commentaries is not different, but here the understanding presented in the two commentaries[85] is not the same.

2.1.11.4. Prayer to enter aeons

> The entering into all future aeons is something
> That I too will do but in merely an instant.
> Whatever the extent of aeons in the three times
> I will act to have entered them in a fraction of an instant.

This is a prayer concerning "*the entering* by buddhas' body, speech, mind, good qualities, and activity *into all* the countless *future aeons* however many there are, whose number, like the number of field atoms of the world realms, is measureless. That entering into the future *is something that I*, by the force of having become a person who also has a bodhisatva's courage, *too will do but in merely* a single *instant*".

Besides that, there is another prayer. "*Whatever the extent of aeons in the three times*"—past, present, and future —is a number of aeons that could not be measured. The mode of entry of the buddhas' body, speech, and mind into the time of that amount of aeons also is not fathomable. "May *I* be able *to act* like that—to have entered the future aeons in their mode—*to have entered them*—that amount of future aeons—*in a fraction of an instant*".

Changkya's commentary says that it is "My mind will enter the amount of aeons in the three times in instants and fractions of an instant, which it will do by the force of wisdom". With that he is saying that this is the complete emancipation of the great

---

[85] These are the commentaries of Adzom Drukpa following Dza Patrul's oral tradition and of Changkya Rolpa'i Dorje.

bodhisatvas[86] who have gained the power to bless an instant into an aeon and to bless an aeon in one instant, and so on, and that this is the sort of entry that must be connected to buddha activity.

How could there be entry in a fraction of an instant into the extent of aeons in the three times? When you have become a buddha, you will have obtained fathomless miracles, and then all entrances of the buddha body, speech, and mind into aeons the amount of the three times will be known through your own all-knowing. Thus, this is a prayer to have the unobstructed miraculous ability to actually be able to enter them in a fraction of an instant. This sort of prayer is designated "a prayer for entry into the matchless, inconceivable arousing of the mind of a bodhisatva of great courage".

2.1.11.5. Entering into viewing the tathagatas

> I will view in a single instant the
> Lions of men gone in the three times.

The ones who have **gone** and will have gone **in the three times** of the past, present, and future, are the conquerors, the complete buddhas, **lions of men**. They referred to as "lions of men" because they are like the king of beasts, the lion, who, when he claims the snowy mountains as his territory, lords over overwhelms the beasts, foxes, monkeys, and so on and cannot be challenged by any of them. The conquerors with their fathomless good qualities such as the set of twenty-one qualities of un-outflowed wisdom—the ten strengths, four non-fears, eighteen unmixed ones, and so on—overwhelm the side not consistent with enlightenment conduct, the māras and their regiments, and cannot be challenged by any of the masses of karma and afflictions. To meet the face of such lions of men or buddhas, you have, as a preliminary, to gather the accumulations and cleanse your obscurations for many aeons. Through that, you will be able to view the fine faces which one cannot get enough of seeing, seeing

---

[86] Great bodhisatvas here meaning those high on the bodhisatva levels.

the countenances of all those adorned with the marks and signs, the lions of men who have gone in the three times, the buddhas whoever they are. "May it be that *I will* suddenly *view* them *in a single instant* of time and from today onwards for an ocean of aeons will not depart from meeting with their faces".

2.1.11.6. Prayer to enter their domain

> I will perpetually enter their domains by
> The force of illusory complete emancipation.

Whenever the domain of inconceivable deeds of those buddhas is looked into, it cannot be measured by rational mind. For example, as with their acting in every instant to protect countless sentient beings from the sufferings of the bad migrations and with their acting in every instant to guide countless sentient beings, ripen them, and liberate them. The conduct named "*illusory*" is about finding certainty in regard to the topic of illusion, which is to realize it in direct perception then manifest it. Manifesting it means that you steer down samsara and nirvana's three paths by means of the samādhi of their being illusory and you have the "*complete emancipation*" or the inconceivable miracles of body, speech, and mind manifested from prajñā and wisdom, and samādhi, referred to as "the deeds of complete emancipation". May it be that *I will perpetually* be able actually to *enter* those inconceivable *domains* of the buddhas, *by the force of* having manifested that sort of meeting the buddhas' faces, a domain of *being illusory* and a domain of being *completely emancipated*. Note that Lochen said, "May I perpetually enter their domain by realizing equipoise's elaboration-free wisdom, with that leading to post-meditation appearing as illusion, whose power then causes complete emancipation from the obscurations, by the force of which I enter."

2.1.11.7. Prayer for entering into intention and production

> Whatever the field arrangements of the three times,
> I will make them manifest on a single atom.

> Like that in all the directions without exception,
> I will enter the arrangements[87] of conquerors' fields.

Just as the bhikṣhu Chokyi Jungnay previously made five hundred great prayers and at the time of the second aeon numbering the sands of the River Ganges gathered accumulations based on which he accomplished the manifestation of the western Sukhāvatī field realm, now I too need to pray that way. It has been taught that, generally speaking, the time when a field is made is at the eighth bodhisatva level. "***Whatever*** ones or those ones that are ***the field arrangements*** however many there are of the inconceivable buddhas ***of the three times***, may ***I*** by the force of my faith, prayers, samādhi, miracles, and so on be able to ***make them manifest on a single atom***." How would you do that? You would do it according to the prayer, "When I have become a buddha in the future and have mastery of miracles, when I use the miracles of more being less and less being more, may I be able accomplish all arrangements of buddha-fields on a single tiny atom." Thus, there is the prayer "***Like that, in all the directions without exception*** of trillions of third-order universes, may I be able to meet in direct perception the delightful ***arrangements*** however many there might be ***of*** the ***conquerors*** of the three times' ***fields***, with their containers and contents[88], supports and supported[89], and not only that but to be to able to ***enter*** meaning engage in the work or act of being able to actually show those in a single instant to all other sentient beings".

---

[87] Tenpa'i Wangchuk's source for Samantabhadra's prayer has the Tibetan term "bkod pa" here in the verse, meaning arrangement, and gives his explanation accordingly. This differs from the edition of the prayer found in the Derge edition of *The Translated Word* in which the term "rgyan" meaning "ornamentation" appears. Arrangement and ornamentation are synonyms for the way that a field is laid out.

[88] Containers are the fields themselves and contents are the beings contained in them.

[89] Supports are the details of the place and supported are the beings living in it.

Changkya Rolpa'i Dorje said that there is a great difference between the earlier "on a single atom …" which concerns viewing the field arrangements of other buddhas, and this, which is the accomplishment of fields by the power of one's own miracles and samādhi, and the actual preparation of a pure field. He said that the latter is available to those on the pure levels, those who have gained the eighth level and up, but for now, for those on the intending concept-based mental levels and the first to seventh bodhisatva levels, it has to be practised with a concentration type of meditation.

2.1.11.8. Prayer to enter going before the tathagatas

> Whichever lamps of the world have not descended
> Will become buddhas at the stage, turn the wheel,
> And show nirvana, the final, utter peace.
> I will go before all those guardians.

"*Whichever*" is a pronoun meaning whoever are the buddhas or *lamps of the world who have not* yet *descended*. They will become the buddhas whose supreme illumination dispels the darkness of ignorance, the sun-like great lamps of the world realms. First they *will* arouse the mind of supreme enlightenment, next train *in the stages of* the conquerors' sons' enlightenment conduct, and at last, when they have manifested complete **buddhahood**, due my having supplicated them to turn the dharma wheel, *turn the wheel* of dharma *and* finally *show*, in the mode of bodily *nirvana, the final, utter peace*[90]. Having emanated my body into bodies equal to the number of field atoms, in order to make a supplication in which they will be urged not to pass into nirvana but to remain for oceans of

---

[90] The correct wording for this line is shown in the verse above. A mistaken tradition of explanation of the words appeared in Tibet several or more centuries ago. The mistaken explanation, which is now universal amongst Tibetans, is seen in this sentence. This wording and with it a mistaken explanation appears in three places in the prayer. The line is fully explained in Nāgārjuna's and my own commentary in volume I.

aeons, *I will go before all those guardians*, the complete buddhas, however many are present, emanating a body in front of each. The "will go" in the last sentence is understood to mean "will be present".

In short, this is a prayer in which, having emanated your own bodies as many in number as however many future buddhas there are, you will urge them to turn the dharma wheel, supplicate them not to pass into nirvana, and so on. Through it, you will become someone who spreads the deeds and enlightened activities of the buddhas to the farthest limits of space.

2.1.12. Prayer for forces

> Forces of miracles which have all speed,
> Forces of vehicle which is in all ways a door,
> Forces of conduct whose quality is always good,
> Force of loving kindnesses which are all pervasive,
>
> Forces of merit which is all virtuous,
> Forces of wisdom become without defilement,
> Forces of prajñā, method, and samādhi—by them
> I'll be truly accomplishing the forces of enlightenment.

Generally speaking "force" has to be understood to mean that which cannot be challenged by anything adverse to it. This has with it a need to pray for the accomplishment, in dependence on nine forces, of the ultimate force of enlightenment or rank of a buddha.

The ***forces of miracles which have all speed*** is the forces of the bodhisatva's miracles that can accomplish what mind desires in an instant. It is like the ability to travel without obstruction to many field realms in an instant and like being able to change an aeon into an instant and an instant into an aeon.

And, "a mode of entry in ***all ways a*** beneficial ***door***, that is, of entry which is in all ways or every way beneficial to all sentient beings", is that whatever you do, it will be beneficial for all sentient beings in various different ways, therefore, having taught inconceivable enumerations of vehicles presenting the holy dharma in conformance with the mental capacity of each one of all sentient beings, there are the *forces of vehicles*, similar to excellent mounts, of arousing the mind.

And, similarly, having yourself *in all* times and circumstances trained in the conduct of bodhisatva Samantabhadra, the conquerors' sons' conduct of the six pāramitās, vast and deep, and not exhaustible, you will have exerted yourself at all doors that become a basis for benefit and ease for all sentient beings, that is, at *the forces of conduct* which are the methods that cause you to connect to the *good qualities*—the ten forces, four non-fears, and so on—of the ultimate, unsurpassed complete buddhahood.

And, being wholly *pervaded* by immeasurable equanimity which is utter evenness without the partiality of attachment or aversion, for *all* migrators whether good, bad, or in-between. And, likewise, being more joyful if other sentient beings have happiness than if oneself has happiness, and having *loving kindnesses* for the infinite sentient beings like a mother has for an only child, and having great compassion for them, there are *the forces of* the four immeasurables.

And *the forces of* all of whatever referenced *merit* has been accumulated in dependence on the generosity, and so on of the conquerors' sons' conducts is karma which is in *all* ways, from beginning to end, *virtuous*.

And, for *the forces of* reference-less *wisdom* which has *become without defilement* or obstruction for all dharmas of the knowable, "forces of wisdom" refers to all appearances of abandonment of what is seen as bad and adoption of what is seen as good being known by the force of wisdom without defilement. Wisdom without defilement is wisdom that has no obscuration or obstruction to its knowing. However, it also refers to the uninterrupted deeds of the permanent, pervasive, and spontaneous, meaning the dharmakāya, done from the state of being without clinging.

And the *force of prajñā* realizes the actuality of all dharmas exactly as it is. And the force of method is that with which the deeds of bodhisatvas skilled in **method** complete in each instant the accumulations of many aeons. *And* the force of **samādhi** is the many hundreds of doors of samādhi—Illusion-Like Samādhi, Going As A Hero Samādhi, Vajra-Like Samādhi, and so on—that the bodhisatvas rely on in order to accomplish all of their qualities. This is the prayer, "May it be that *I will* be able, based on the good qualities that come from the nine types of force, to ***truly accomplish the forces of*** the ultimate result, the rank of great complete ***enlightenment***".

As explained above, "force" refers to any special method that cannot be overpowered or affected by anything of the adverse side, and to special prajñā and special samādhi.

2.1.13. Prayer for accomplishing the antidote

> Wholly purifying the forces of karma,
> Totally destroying the forces of affliction, and
> Utterly rendering powerless the forces of māra,
> The forces of excellent conduct will be completed.

I will be ***wholly purifying the forces of karma*** that propel me into samsara—the ten non-virtuous karmas, the five immediate ones, the five proximate to those, the four heavy ones, the eight wrong ones, and so on. As well as those, I will be wholly purifying transgressions of the outer vows of personal emancipation, the inner trainings of the bodhisatva, and the secret mantra samayas of the vidyādharas. Furthermore, I will be wholly purifying transgressions of abjuring worldly oaths, competing in worldly ways, lack of shame and propriety, and so on. I will be wholly purifying all non-virtuous karmas that I have accumulated by applying their antidotes to my mindstream, for example, anger's antidote the practise of patience, desire's antidote the observation of the ugly, delusions's antidote meditation on absorption, and so on.

And I will be ***totally destroying the forces of affliction***. The forces of affliction are the groups of afflictions both subtle and coarse—the five root afflictions, the twenty proximate afflictions, the fifty mental events, the eighty-four thousand-fold group of thoughts, and so on. I will wholly destroy or defeat them by sending the army of antidotes that will get rid of them.

And, I will be ***utterly rendering powerless the forces of māra***—the māras Garab Wangchuk[91] and the others and their māra regiments, and furthermore, the māra of the aggregates, the māra of the lord of death, the māra of the son of the gods, and so on. I will render them powerless or forceless by applying the antidote, for example, defeating the māra of the aggregates by realizing the lack of truth in the aggregates, defeating the māra of the lord of death by realizing mindness to be free of production and disintegration, and defeating the māra of the son of the gods by purification of clinging to my homeland.

The forces of excellent conduct will be completed. I will train in the ocean-like aspects of enlightenment conduct by completing an ocean-like accumulation of the two accumulations, ripening ocean-like numbers of those to be tamed, purifying ocean-like field realms, and so on. And, having finalized that threefold completing, ripening, and purifying, I will have completed the forces of enlightenment conduct. Thus, this is praying that, "Through those means, may it be that I will gain the rank of a buddha".

2.1.14. Prayer for enlightened activity

> I will be completely purifying an ocean of fields,
> Completely liberating the ocean of sentient beings,
> Utterly seeing an ocean of dharmas,
> Utterly realizing an ocean of wisdom,

---

[91] Garab Wangchuk is the equivalent of cupid.

Completely purifying an ocean of conduct,
Wholly completing an ocean of prayers,
Utterly offering to an ocean of buddhas,
And doing so tirelessly for an ocean of aeons.

I will make all these appearing container worlds, the *field* realms pervading where there is space, vast and great in number as the atoms in *an ocean*, into something *completely pure* with grounds of precious substance, trees, flowers, lakes, and so on, like the western Sukhāvatī field, and so delightful that one cannot get enough of seeing them. That is the prayer "May I be able to make such a container wholly pure". May I be able to *make* the *sentient beings* as great in number as the *oceans* of them contained in the container of the becomings *completely liberated* from the various sufferings of karma and afflictions, and so on. May I gain the eye of prajñā that views the entire excellent speech, which is like *an ocean* of *dharmas* of scripture and realization and makes *utterly seen* the topics of acceptance and rejection. In other words, may I see them. Then, may I be able to realize the actuality of all dharmas, phenomena, in direct perception by the wisdom which knows the actuality of phenomena and to realize clearly and without mixup all the knowable phenomena by the wisdom which sees the extent, and so through the forces of producing such ocean-like wisdoms in my mindstream *make an ocean of wisdom utterly realized*.

"*May I make an ocean of conduct completely pure*". For as long as the masses of karma and affliction of the mindstreams of the infinite sentient beings has not ended, I will purify an ocean of bodhisatva conduct for the sake of those sentient beings; I will completely purify all of the side not conducive to enlightenment conduct, the stains of bad mind which thinks of its own sake. May I *make*, for the purpose of shaking out the deep pit of three-realmed samsara, *an ocean of prayers* so that I also will, as happened with the prayer festival of one million two hundred thousand great prayers and Bhikṣhu Chokyi Jungnay's five hundred great prayers, *wholly complete* all the results that come from making prayers. This is the prayer "May the results of prayer be accomplished. May I accomplish my purpose in making prayers, with all results prayed for becoming wholly completed". May I *utterly* make *offerings* to *an ocean* of countless *buddhas* with clouds of offerings like Samantabhadra's cloud of offering. The above set of seven virtuous acts—pure fields, and so on—must be done for an ocean of aeons but must be done as a hero acting out of courage, not with a cowering mindstream, thus, *I will* happily be *doing so tirelessly for an ocean of aeons*.

2.1.15. Prayer for training following

2.1.15.1. Prayer to train following the buddhas

> The conquerors gone in the three times had their
> Particular prayers of enlightenment conduct;
> Becoming an enlightened buddha by excellent conduct,
> I will complete all their prayers without exception.

There are who are *the* countless fathomless *conquerors gone in the three times*. Prior to attaining buddhahood when they had entered the path of training, they aroused the thought—the mind of supreme enlightenment. Then, when they were training in the fathomless topics of the conquerors' sons' conduct—the conducts of generosity, and so on—they made inconceivable amounts of *their* own *particular prayers*—such as the five hundred great prayers—*of enlightenment conduct*. Now, I who also have aroused the excellent thought—the mind for supreme enlightenment—and have done the excellent conduct—the conduct of the conquerors' sons—during many aeons, will in the future *become an enlightened buddha* at the level of unsurpassed supreme enlightenment based on that *excellent conduct*. At that time, I will have brought to fruition every one without exception of the entire extent of prayers that the buddhas of the three times have made in the past. This then is a prayer "May it be that *I will complete all of* the conquerors' specific prayers, whatever they were, without exception".

2.1.15.2. Prayers to train following the two supreme bodhisatvas
2.1.15.2.1. Prayer to train following Samantabhadra

> The chief of the sons of all the conquerors is
> The one whose name is "Samantabhadra"—
> I utterly dedicate all these virtues here in order
> To conduct myself with expertise equalling his.
>
> The way he is expert at excellent dedications for
> Completely pure body, speech, and mind, and
> Completely pure conduct, and wholly pure fields,
> May I too be equal to him in the same way.

According to Patrul Rinpoche's oral tradition, "*the chief son*", means the supreme son among the sons *of all the conquerors* of the three times and that Samantabhadra "was senior to them in four ways: years, training, good qualities, and wisdom". He *is the one whose name is* bodhisatva "*Samantabhadra*". He has become supremely expert like that because of having comprehended the ocean-like dharma element[92], so it says, "*in order to conduct myself with expertise equalling* or the same as *his*". How should I be equal to him? There is the prayer "*I* will *utterly dedicate all of these virtues here* to being able to arouse the mind of supreme enlightenment in the same way as bodhisatva Samantabhadra does, to gathering an ocean of the two accumulations through training in the conquerors' sons' conduct as he does, and to finalizing the three of completing, ripening, and purifying as he does".

Furthermore, there is the question "How would I train in bodhisatva Samantabhadra's conduct?" He showed his *completely pure body* in various forms to those to be tamed; as Jigmey Lingpa said:

> May various forms be used to tame migrators:
> Low, high, and sick dharma teachers,

---

[92] The dharma element is one of the eighteen dhātus or elements. It is the entire spread of phenomena or dharmas known to mind.

And birds, gentle creatures, and city beggars
Shown in order to tame as needed.

And Śhāntideva said:

May I be an island for those wanting an island,
A lamp for those wanting a lamp,
A bed for those wanting a bed,
And a totally subservient slave for
Those wanting a slave.

Similarly, the completely pure *speech* teaches dharma to all migrators via various languages, as was said earlier with "languages of gods, nāgas ..." ***And also*** the completely pure *mind* enters many hundreds of thousands of different doors of samādhi. ***Completely pure conduct*** cannot be overwhelmed by the things of the side not conducive to the conquerors' conduct—the six pāramitās and so on—not even by subtle bad actions and downfalls. ***Wholly pure fields*** is that all containers and contents are, like the Sukhāvatī field, the nature only of purity. Based on those former five purities, there is the making of the complete purity in every instant of the perfection of the containers and contents comprising the buddha-fields, so a dedication made for the purpose of gaining that set of five purities is an ***excellent dedication*** or one which is best or supreme amongst all dedications. If we then ask who makes an excellent dedication like that, the answer is that it is the one with ***expertise***, Samantabhadra. Thus "***May I too be equal to him***, the great bodhisatva Samantabhadra, able to make dedications ***in the same way*** as he does".

2.1.15.2.2. Prayer to train following Manjughosha

For thoroughly virtuous excellent conduct
I will act as in the prayer of Mañjushrī.
Without wearying in all future aeons
I will complete their works without exception.

In order to perform the ***excellent conduct*** of that especially noble path of joined method and prajñā which is ***thoroughly***—from beginning to end and at all times— ***virtuous—I will act*** in the same way ***as in the prayer*** made by the great bodhisatva noble ***Mañjuśhrī*** through great courage, so I too, in order to produce a ***prayer*** of that sort through all my doors, condensing the forces of body, speech, and mind into one, ***will act*** with intense resolve and from the core of my heart in the enlightened conduct. That much is training following Mañjuśhrīghoṣha.

Now, the buddhas of the ten directions and the great bodhisatvas first arouse the mind of supreme enlightenment, then at the time of training in the conquerors' sons' conduct have the approach of arousing courage. It is necessary to do the vast, deep, and long-running ocean-like enlightenment conduct ***in all*** of countless ***future aeons*** with its difficult tasks of performing the generosity of head and limbs, but there can be no cowering and ***no wearying*** of mind. There can only be the heroic approach of entering it with great pleasure like geese coming down to a lake adorned with lotuses or children entering a grove of flowers and fruit trees or elephants oppressed by heat entering a pool of water without hesitation—that is the way the bodhisatvas of great courage enter enlightenment conduct. That being so there is the prayer, "***I*** too at the time of training in enlightenment conduct ***will*** do ***the works*** of enlightenment conduct just exactly as the buddhas, the two chief sons[93], and the bodhisatvas before me have trained in them. For the sake of all the infinite sentient beings, during an ocean of aeons and even though I will have to perform the generosity of giving head and limbs, I will, without holding back from having courage, wholly ***complete*** all the enlightenment conduct ***without exception***".

At this point, the prayers of the main part of *Excellent Conduct* are complete.

---

[93] ... Mañjuśhrī and Samantabhadra ...

Section 3

The Virtue of the End, The Concluding Topics of the Text

2.1.16. Concluding dedication

> May my conducts not become measurable.
> May my good qualities also be immeasurable.
> Due to remaining in conduct without measure
> I will gain all of their transformations.

This is praying, "The bodhisatva's completely pure conduct is vast and deep, like an ocean, therefore, its extent or measure is not something that can be grasped so *"may my pure conduct not come to have a measure"*[94]. Similarly, the good qualities arising from the bodhisatva's conduct—retentions, knowledgeability, and inconceivable three secrets of a bodhisatva's body, speech, and mind—do not have a measure that is measurable by dualistic mind. For example, the twelve sets of one hundred good qualities of the first level, the twelve thousand sets of good qualities of the second level, and so on do not have an measure that could be grasped mentally. Therefore,

---

[94] The wording here comes from a mistaken explanation that appeared with the later Tibetan commentators. The Tibetan phrasing here "spyod pa dag" can mean either "pure conduct" or "conducts". The Indian masters such as Nāgārjuna say that it must be understood as "conducts".

may my good qualities also be immeasurable, meaning without a measure that could be assessed. In that way, even though I come *to remain* on the high levels where the bodhisatva's *measureless conduct* and measureless good qualities have been gained, *I will* for the sakes of all migrator sentient beings *gain all* however many there are *of* the inconceivable miracles and good qualities which arise as *their*—those buddhas and bodhisatvas'—*transformations* of body, speech, and mind". Here, the Tibetan word " 'tshal"[95] translated with "gain" can have many meanings such as "gain", "know", "exist", and so on, but in this case has to be understood to have the meaning "gain".

At this point the sixteen topics have been completed and the explanation of the actual divisions of the prayer is finished.

2.2. Showing the end of the prayer

> As far as it would be to the final end of space
> And to the end of every sentient being likewise,
> And as much as to the end of karma and affliction,
> It will also be that much to the end of my prayer.

Nobody can fathom how *far it would be to the final end of space* because it is impossible for there to be an end of space. *And*, given that where space pervades sentient beings pervade, *to the end of every sentient being* of the six classes of migrator *likewise*, meaning that sentient beings also have the same end or reach as space; in

---

[95] The Indian commentaries say that this term which in Tibetan is " 'tshal ba" has five meanings and that the meaning here is "to know" in the sense of the time arriving at which one knows that one has gained them. Those commentaries also point out that "gain", can be understood as the meaning here but that "come to know" is the literal meaning intended. Unfortunately, later Tibetan commentators dropped the subtlety of that earlier explanation and simply stated that it means "to gain", which is what has happened here with the system of explanation descended from Dza Patrul.

other words, sentient beings' presence is unending. *And*, given that that is the amount of sentient beings, *as much as* it would be *to the end of* the ***karma and affliction*** in their mindstreams also has no end. Until karma and affliction end, ***my prayer*** as an antidote to that karma and affliction ***also*** be without end or will go on for ***that much***.

In short, this prayer is saying "Where space pervades, sentient beings also pervade, and where sentient beings pervade, karma and afflictions pervade, and where karma and afflictions pervade, unsatisfactoriness pervades; everywhere that unsatisfactoriness pervades, may its opponent, that which will dispel it, my prayer of enlightenment conduct, pervade. For as long as space does not finish, as long as sentient beings do not finish, as long as karma and affliction do not finish, as long as unsatisfactoriness does not finish, may my prayer also not finish and in not finishing become the actual antidote that dispels the suffering of migrators pervasive as space is." It is like what the conquerors' son Śhāntideva said:

> For as long as space remains and
> For as long as sentient beings remain
> For that long may I remain and
> Dispel migrators' unsatisfactoriness.

2.3. Showing the advantages then concluding

This is the two parts of the prayer's advantages and the dedication of the prayer having those advantages.

2.3.1. The prayer's advantages
2.3.1.1. The synopsis

> Compared to one who adorns the infinite fields wherever
>   in the ten directions
> With jewels and offers that to the conquerors,

And offers the most enjoyable things of gods and men
For aeons as many as the atoms of the fields,

The one who hears this king of dedications
Then is utterly inspired towards and even just one time
Gives rise to faith in supreme enlightenment
Is the one who has the better superior merits.

Considering the roots of merit of *someone who adorns the infinite*—their vastness being hard to measure with rational mind—boundless, limitless universe *fields wherever in the ten directions* and fills them to overflowing *with* various *jewels and* then *offers that to the conquerors* of the ten directions and three times, *and* not only that but the merit gained when that person *offers* however many are *the most enjoyable things of gods and men* such as beautiful visual forms, sweet sounds, good smells, sweet tastes, smooth touches, and so on, *for* a duration of *aeons as many as the atoms of the fields* of the world realms of the ten directions to the buddhas and bodhisatvas, how could anyone measure that? *Compared to* that, if *someone who hears this king of dedications*, this *King of Prayers of Excellent Conduct*, with his ears and has a good understanding of the meaning *then*, knowing that the result of this prayer is that all sentient beings, self and others, will have the rank of supreme unsurpassed great enlightenment, in a state of rejoicing *is utterly inspired towards* and with joy *even just one time* utterly *gives rise to faith in* the conduct ocean-like in its aspects of *supreme enlightenment* and with that makes a deep prayer from the depths of his heart, the merit he will have will be much more noble than the former merit or will be *the better* of the two *superior merits*[96]. It is so because, for as long as the pit of this three-realmed samsara has to be shaken out, that is, for as long as there has not been an end to the sentient beings of the three realms, the result of this prayer also will not be finished.

---

[96] There are many kinds of merit. "Superior merit" is the kind that is connected with gaining emancipation from samsara.

2.3.1.2. Full explanation

> Someone one who has made this excellent conduct prayer

This is the start of thirteen benefits taught for reciting the prayer. **Someone**—a person of faith, devotion, and trust—**who has** nicely **made this excellent conduct prayer** by keeping thought and action synchronized so that the meanings shown in this prayer were both recited and brought to mind, will have gained thirteen benefits as follows.

> 1) Will have abandoned bad migrations,

Someone who has recited this while keeping his mind on the meaning **will have abandoned all** of any bad karmas he might have accumulated that would send him to one of the **bad migrations**. From today on he will pass through a succession of good bodies in the good migrations which will definitely end in gaining the rank of a buddha.

> 2) He will have abandoned bad companions,

Someone who has exerted himself from the depths of his heart at this excellent conduct prayer from today on until he has gained the rank of great enlightenment *will* not meet with bad company, persons of evil deeds. Even if he does, not falling under that person's influence, he also **will have** swiftly **abandoned** such **bad companions** with their evil deeds.

> 3) And he will also see Amitābha soon.

Moreover, that person who has made effort from his heart at this prayer will not only have abandoned bad migrations and companions of evil deeds but in this life even **will soon see** buddha **Amitābha** decorated with the marks and signs, and, at the time of his death, will in the intermediary state have Amitābha surrounded by a retinue of a fathomless assembly of bodhisatva bhikshus and sangha descend in direct perception before him, with music resounding from the heavens and a path of rainbow light shown, a rain of flowers coming ahead to presage and coming behind to follow, which is the way he travels in western Sukhāvatī field. As Chagmey Rinpoche said:

> Emanated buddha Amitābha
> Surrounded by bhikṣhu and saṅgha retinues
> Please descend before me in direct perception.

4) They acquire the best,

What those persons who exert themselves at this prayer *acquire* is an unsurpassed acquisition, one which is *the best* of most excellent acquisitions. Saying that it is like the acquisition of a wish-fulfilling jewel which is a supreme acquisition because it removes poverty in this life, does not afford a good comparison. Saying that it is like a person who has acquired the wealth and possessions of the three realms also does not afford a good comparison. This is so because when someone exerts himself at the meaning shown in this *Excellent Conduct Prayer*, he acquires the attainment of the precious rank of unsurpassed complete buddhahood and there is there is no better, more excellent acquisition than that to be found in the world realms.

5) are sustained in goodness,

Generally speaking, "*sustained in goodness*" is a metaphor for what is the cause for this prayer to be accomplished, which is that you definitely must have the three things: keeping pure discipline; gathering vast accumulations; and making connections with completely pure prayers. If you have those three, whatever sickness, negative forces, or bad circumstances arise for you, their various bad circumstances appear as assistants, turning into the cause of the bodhisatva's body and mind both being sustained in happiness.

6) And even in this human life can turn out well.

If that person exerts himself at the meaning shown—the advice for conquerors' sons contained in *A King of Prayers of Excellent Conduct*—and makes stainless prayers accordingly, then, without even needing to speak of the string of future lives that he will pass through and finally reach emancipation and at the rank of all-knowing, *even in*

this human life there will be: blessings of all buddhas and bodhisatvas; long life, absence of sickness, and plans accomplished without obstacles; removal of circumstances counter to the accomplishment of the holy dharma and enlightenment; all circumstances conducive to it produced without effort; the basis for all good types of benefit and ease planted; and so for him happiness and goodness can come. In other words, his life ***can turn out well***.

7) Moreover, whatever Samantabhadra is like,
Before long they will become like that too.

There are the persons who perform the *Prayer of Excellent Conduct* whoever they might be. There is bodhisatva **Samantabhadra** with his good qualities of arousal of the enlightenment mind, good qualities of conduct, capabilities at miracles, and so on, however many they are, as seen long ago by youthful Sudhana when he was "able to enter into the ocean-like maṇḍala of Samantabhadra". Samantabhadra accepted Sudhana and told him, "***Moreover, whatever*** my good qualities are ***like, before long they will become like that too***". What actually happened at the time was explained earlier in the prefatory material which laid out the circumstances surrounding the prayer—Samantabhadra put his hand on Youthful Sudhana's head then said the words of this couplet:

Moreover, whatever Samantabhadra is like,
Before long they will become like that too.

8) The evil deeds of the five immediates done
By someone under the control of not knowing will
If he recites this excellent conduct prayer,
Be quickly and without exception wholly cleansed.

The Buddha said that five particular actions, which he called "the five immediate karmas" are, karmically speacking, the worst possible actions that can be done. They cause the person who has done any of them to fall into hell as soon as the breath ends at death. "Immediate" means both that there is no rebirth taken after that life before falling into hell and that there is also no intermediary state between that death and rebirth. In short, having done one of these, one goes directly into birth in the hell of Unending Torment, falling into it like a stone dropped from a high place. The five immediates are: killing one's father; killing one's mother; killing an arhat; drawing blood from the body of the tathāgata with a negative mind; and causing a schism in the saṅgha. There are no greater evil acts in the worldly realms than *the evil deeds of the five immediates*. These very great evils that have been *done by* some ordinary being *under the control of* the stupidity of *not knowing will be quickly and without exception wholly cleansed, if he recites this excellent conduct prayer* again and again with complete sincerity while laying them aside from the depths of his heart using the four forces of antidote.

When doing the prayer, you must remain undistracted by words and thoughts! However, if you recite without thinking anything at all, it will not be possible for the cleansing to happen. Therefore, it is very important to think about the meanings contained in this prayer as you recite it. It is like the oral advice given by Dodrupchen Jigmey Tennyi:

> It is important to make effort at the excellent conduct prayer. Reciting it is not the main thing. Contemplating it is the main thing.

In general, reading the sutras while contemplating their meaning is the way to cleanse evil deeds. However, it says in *Zhamar's Stages of the Path*:

> Previously a bhikṣhu in the U Tsang region sold twelve bundles of the Prajñāpāramitā, then later saw this was as bad as hawking up phlegm and spitting it on the Excellent Word, so with regretful mind made hundreds of full-length prostrations with recitations of the prayer equivalent to reading it many times. On the verge of his death, he saw a vision of birth in hell with the henchmen of death rushing in to get him, loudly roaring "Kill! Strike!" Knowing that this was the result of selling the Prajñāpāramitā texts, he

saw himself doing the full-length prostrations and recitations, and all of the holy figures connected with it appeared before him, at which point he died. For him, the benefits of reciting the sutras needed to be experienced no more than that much!

Thus, reading this excellent conduct prayer while contemplating its meanings has inconceivable benefits. Similarly, there is nothing better than reciting the sutras for giving birth in your mindstream to a special kind of prajñā which has mastery over threefold hearing, contemplating, and meditating. Previously, there was the leader among conquerors Longchen Rabjam who had inconceivable latencies of training done in many past lifetimes. There was also the second actual conqueror[97], who was a person of primordial buddhahood but who, taking the appearance of someone to be tamed, read the *Eight Thousand Verse Prajñāpāramitā Sutra* one hundred times. He said that the blessings of the teachings in the sutras caused the view of actuality to be born in his mindstream, together with a vast utter knowledge which knew the entirety of knowables without obstruction. Similarly, other previous holy ones purified all evil deeds without exception through reciting the great sutras and there are stories of past events that show their attainment of inconceivable good qualities.

9) He will possess wisdom, form,
   Marks, family, and colour.

The person who makes this prayer ***will*** give birth in his mindstream and so come to ***possess*** within his life the no-thought ***wisdom*** of the path of seeing that sees the actuality of dharmas as it is.

10) The person who exerts himself at this excellent conduct prayer will in all of his successive lives possess a ***form*** so perfect and lovely to behold that it will steal away the minds of the nine types of

---

[97] ... Padmasambhava ...

beings[98] and in future will gain the appearance of the fine form of a buddha's nirmāṇakāya ornamented with the thirty-two excellent *marks* and the eighty excellent illustrative signs. And that person will possess a perfect *family* line—such as the family lines of kings, priests, accomplished ones, and realized ones, where father and mother follow dharma. And the original Sanskrit says that the person will possess "varṇa" which is "*colour*"[99] in English, meaning that his body will be radiant with good lustre and complexion. That person will come to possess various good qualities such as the ones just listed.

11) Many māras and Tīrthikas will be unable to affect him;

Many attacks of *māras* and māra regiments, *and* as well as that outsider *Tīrthikas* with their wrong views, and so on *will be unable to* have a harmful *affect* on the person who makes this prayer. Such things will not even find the opportunity to do so.

That being so, no matter which external obstacles of māras and their māra regiments you might have and which internal obstacles of evil deeds and obscuration there are in your own mindstream, if you exert yourself at this prayer connected with the motivation of the excellent thought of enlightenment mind and with the excellent conduct coming from it of the conquerors' sons' conduct—generosity and so on—then, as in the example of travelling while accompanied by a group of heroic escorts, no enemy attack will be able to inflict harm on you. No attacker will be able to affect you. Śhāntideva said:

---

[98] The nine types of beings are three types each of the beings in the desire, form, and formless realms. Here, it is simply a way of saying "all sentient beings of all types".

[99] The Sanskrit term literally means colour, but is also used to indicate "complexion" in the same way that the English word "colour" is used to indicate the state of a person's complexion.

Although I have done exceptionally unbearable evil,
If like relying on a hero in the face of great fears
This is relied on, I will quickly go past it.[100]
Why then do the conscientious ones not rely on this?

12) In all three worlds even offerings will be made to him.

A person who has exerted himself in both thought and action at this *Prayer of Excellent Conduct* becomes worthy of having prostrations and offerings made to him by all the gods and men—chief of whom are Devendra, Brahmā, and the wheel-wielding kings who rule over men, and so on. And those residing **in all three worlds even**—below the earth, on top of the earth, and above the earth—that is, in all realms, will see him as a suitable place for all gods and men to prostrate and so **make offerings to him**.

Why is that? The person who arouses the mind of supreme enlightenment, trains in the excellent conduct to be trained in by bodhisatvas, and makes prayers like this one will, from that today on in his lifetime, even if he had till then been known as a scared, timid person reviled by everyone, be given the new name, "a son of the sugatas". From then on he will be seen in a different light as someone worthy of being prostrated to by all the gods and men of the world. *Entering the Conduct* says:

> If the enlightenment mind has been produced, in one instant
> The scared ones locked in the prison of samsara
> Will be called "a son of the sugatas" and
> Will be objects of prostration by the world with its gods and men.

13) He'll quickly go to the foot of the leading bodhi tree
And, having done so, in order to benefit sentient beings,

---

[100] "This" refers to the enlightenment mind.

Will sit there, become an enlightened buddha, utterly
   turn the wheel,
And tame all the māras together with their regiments.

The person who keeps this *Prayer of Excellent Conduct* in mind and practises what is shown in it **will quickly** complete the journey through the levels and paths, then **go to** sit at **the foot of the leading** tree, the **bodhi tree. And, having done so, in order to** bring **benefit** and ease to all **sentient beings** by gaining the precious rank of an enlightened, unsurpassed complete buddha, **will sit there** with legs crossed up in the vajra posture with that bodhi tree as his back rest. Like the previous buddha, Śhākyamuni, he will say:

   For as long as I have not gained enlightenment
   For that long I will not break my posture.

and will remain there attuned to dharma. Then he will attain unsurpassed **enlightenment**, becoming a manifest complete **buddha.** And then, in order to **utterly turn the wheel** of dharma of the three vehicles for those who belong to one of the families of disciples addressed by those three wheels, he will use the antidotes of the Vajra-Like and Loving Kindness samādhis to **tame all the māras together with their regiments.** Previously, when the Buddha Bhagavat was becoming a buddha, he tamed the māras in the first period of the night, entered equipoise at midnight, and in the earliest part of the morning while beating the victory drum became a manifest complete buddha, fulfilling both his own and others' aims.

2.3.1.3. The meaning summed up through benefits

   For whoever holds, reads or teaches
   This prayer of excellent conduct
   Their full-ripenings will be known by buddha.
   Do not be sceptical of supreme enlightenment!

Some person **whoever** it is who **holds** the letters of **this prayer of excellent conduct**—best would be written out in precious substances such as gold, silver, etcetera, otherwise in vermillion ink, etcetera, then nicely wrapped and bound—on his body, or someone else who *reads* it aloud while remembering the meaning as he says the words or reads it for others *or teaches* its words and meanings to others, the benefits of those roots of merit or *their full-ripenings will be* inconceivable, *known* only to the wisdom of a complete *buddha.* If the others—the shrāvakas, pratyekabuddhas, and bodhisatvas—were to discuss it for many aeons even, they would not be able to express it!

You ordinary beings! *Do not* because of lacking trust *be sceptical* or doubtful *of* this *supreme* path that will accomplish the total knowledge of *enlightenment.* You should not be sceptical about it! Why not? Because even if the sun and moon in the sky could fall to the ground, the ṛiṣhi[101] who speaks the truth could not possibly speak falsely.

2.3.2. Dedication of the prayer with benefits (dedication of having kept, written, and recited while keeping the meaning in mind this prayer)

2.3.2.1. Dedication in connection with the great bodhisatvas Manjushri and Samantabhadra

> How the hero Mañjushrī knows
> And Samantabhadra who is like that too;
> In order to train following them,
> I will utterly dedicate all of these virtues.

Generally speaking, as it says in a commentary to *Entering the Middle Way*, the whole meaning of this excellent conduct prayer when condensed down will be contained in these four lines.

How the bodhisatva *hero* Noble *Mañjushrī knows* is that he knows how it is, the suchness of the profound actuality of superfactual truth, and that he knows all the phenomena however many there are, all the dharmas of fictional truth, clearly and without mixup, like

---

[101] That is, Shākyamuni Buddha.

putting fresh Myrobalan in the hand[102]. Based on that, he is someone of great courage that never shrinks from liberating all of the infinite sentient beings from the sufferings general and specific of samsara, that is, he is an heroic being. **And** there is the bodhisatva ***Samantabhadra who is*** exactly ***like that*** Noble Mañjuśrī ***too***—there is nothing of their two knowledges just described nor of their courage to carry the burden of others' sakes that does not match. Therefore, you decide to follow them in every way. ***In order to train following*** those two noble ones and the other bodhisatvas however many there are in every way, you arouse the mind of supreme enlightenment as they did, arouse great courage like theirs, and then train in the bodhisatva's path as they did. You ***utterly dedicate all of these virtues*** made in reciting the prayer to that.

2.3.2.2. Entering into conquerors' dedications or entering how the buddhas would pray

> Using the dedication which all the conquerors
> Gone in the three times commend as supreme
> I utterly dedicate all these roots of virtue of mine
> For the purpose of excellent conduct.

Using that ***dedication which all the conquerors***—the ones who have ***gone*** to complete buddhahood ***in the three times***—and the assembly of their sons the bodhisatvas with one mind and one voice ***commend as supreme*** ... That dedication is a dedication which, made through unified emptiness and compassion is free from grasping at the three spheres. Using that sort I dedication, ***I*** too ***utterly dedicate all these roots of virtue of mine*** that I have accumulated through: development stage practise of a deity, recitation of texts, mantra recitation, prostration, circumambulation, cleansing obscurations, threefold hearing, contemplating, and meditating, and even the tiniest virtues such as a small monk giving a morsel of food to a crow. Thus, you

---

[102] A Myrobalan is a fruit with a most unusual texture. When you see it in your hand, you see all sorts of aspects to it at once.

utterly dedicate all your roots of virtue of the three times *for the purpose of* all sentient beings infinite as space gaining the unsurpassed total knowledge of a truly complete buddha through the *excellent conduct* of enlightenment done just as the noble Samantabhadra practised it.

2.3.2.3. Dedication for the result of the prayer to be manifest

> When the time has come for me to die,
> May all obscurations clear away;
> Seeing Amitābha in direct perception,
> I will utterly go to the field of Sukhāvatī.
>
> Having gone there, may all these prayers
> Without exception become manifest.
> Having completely fulfilled them without exception,
> I will benefit sentient beings as long as the world.

One day, *when the time has come for me to die may all* the *obscurations* I have accumulated—heavy karmas such as the five immediates, rejection of dharma, and so on, and all other karmas, and afflictions, evil deeds, obscurations, latencies, and so on—*clear* as though thrown far *away* as a result of having exerted myself at this *Prayer of Excellent Conduct*. *Seeing*, at that time or later on in the intermediary state, the buddha *Amitābha*, whose name means Infinite Illumination, *in direct perception* together with his retinue of an unfathomable number of bodhisatva bhikshus wearing the three robes and a wonderful arrangement of golden flowers come to escort me to his buddha-field, I will go with them. While seeing the body of Amitābha, he speaks to soothe me, considering me with his mind of great love, "Hey there, son of the family! Do not be scared, do not be afraid! We have come forth to lead you to Sukhāvatī". Then *I will utterly go* together with all of them and in an instant *to the field of Sukhāvatī*.

Having gone there, inside the enclosure of a lotus flower made of precious substances and in an instant by a miracle of mind, a fully developed body is produced[103] and you acquire the supreme body of a bodhisatva having the marks and illustrative signs. The lotus flower opens and immediately you see the countenance of the guardian Amitābha's face. The obscurations to be abandoned on the path of seeing are purified immediately and you gain the first bodhisatva level, Utter Joy. You are immediately able to engage in the one million, two hundred thousand prayers, and so on, therefore, you have made as many *prayers* as are made within this *Prayer of Excellent Conduct*. The result of *these* prayers without exception becomes manifest, so the result for one's own sake, the dharmakāya, has been manifested and the result for others' sakes, *all* the aims *without exception* of all migrators pervading the limits of space, *has been manifested. May* this be accomplished!

The dharmakāya having become manifest like that, may *I* alone, without needing to rely on anyone else, be able to *completely fulfill* the aims *without exception* of those prayers. With that there is the prayer that, having done that, *I* alone *will* accomplish both all types of the temporary *benefit* and ultimate ease of all *sentient beings* for *as long as the world* of the boundless universes of third-order worlds, that is, this three-realmed samsara, has not been emptied.

2.3.2.4. Dedication or prayer to actually obtain the prophecy from a buddha

> In that good and pleasing maṇḍala of the conqueror
> May I be born from an exceptionally beautiful fine lotus.
> Seeing conqueror Amitābha directly,
> May I also obtain the prophecy there.

The maṇḍala which has arisen as an arrangement produced because of the body, speech, and mind, and the miracles of knowledge, love, and capacity of Guardian Amitābha, conqueror over the armies of

---

[103] This refers to miraculous birth, which is one of the four types of birth.

the four māras or complete conqueror over all things not conducive to enlightenment, is the field realm of Sukhāvatī with its completely pure container and pure contents. The container aspect has an extremely *good* arrangement, being adorned with a ground made of precious substances, a wish-fulfilling tree, a river of water of the eight excellent aspects, various beautiful and lovely flowers, and so on. And, the contained sentient beings enjoy the Great Vehicle dharma which they like, so it is a very pleasing and exceptionally delightful place. *In that good and pleasing maṇḍala of the conqueror, may I be born* in the miraculous type of birth *from a* perfect lotus flower made wholly of the seven precious substances. It will be of *exceptionally beautiful* shape and colour, a *fine lotus* with fathomless good qualities, lovely to behold. Immediately on being born in it, I will *see* the countenance which one cannot get enough of seeing of the buddha Infinite Illumination or *conqueror Amitābha directly*. For his speech, I will be able to enjoy whichever is pleasing to me of his many oral instructions. One day, when I have gained the eighth level and it is time for the prophecy, Guardian Amitābha will extend his right arm like an elephant's trunk and, putting it on my head, will say, "Son of the family! You in the future at such and such time will become a buddha, in such and such sort of field realm, as such and such buddha". Thus it says, *"may I also obtain the prophecy* for supreme enlightenment *there"*.

2.3.2.5. Having obtained the prophecy, a prayer to accomplish benefit for sentient beings

> Having completely obtained the prophecy there,
> I will with many emanations, thousands of millions,
> By force of mind, throughout the ten directions
> Do many things to benefit sentient beings.

Having completely obtained such *prophecy there* in that western field of Sukhāvatī, having accomplished for myself in that place a mass of perfect good qualities such as having mastery over prayers, samādhis, miracles, and so on, *I will with* a great *many emanations—thousands of millions* meaning infinitely many—work in many ways to benefit sentient beings. Moreover, I will, *by* the great *force of mind* that I will possess concerned only with the sake of others and not in the slightest with my own and by the force of both method and prajñā pāramitās, do many things to benefit sentient beings *throughout the* world realms of the *ten directions* however many there are. This is a dedication saying, "May I *do many things to benefit* the infinite *sentient beings* for as long as they have not been liberated from the all the sufferings of samsara, for as long as they have not gained unsurpassed total knowledge, the precious rank of a truly complete buddha. For as long as samsara has not been emptied, may I do the acts of the permanent, pervasive, and spontaneous[104] by showing those sentient beings emanations to tame them as needed".

Next, there are two prayers which have been added as later additions: a dedication of the roots of merit of having recited this excellent conduct prayer; and a dedication of the results of the prayer to others.[105]

The first is a dedication of the roots of merit of having recited this excellent conduct prayer:

> May the trifle of virtue accumulated by the one
> Who has recited this excellent conduct prayer
> Cause the virtues of migrators' prayers
> To be obtained by them all in an instant.

May the trifle of roots of *virtue accumulated*—no matter how small, even such as giving some food to a frightened insect—by having *recited this excellent conduct prayer* with my own speech or having made others recite it *cause the virtues* that will be the results *of migrators'* good sorts of prayers whatever each one has made, *to be*

---

[104] These three things are qualities of and hence stand in for saying "dharmakāya".

[105] There is some doubt over this, as discussed in the introduction.

obtained by each of *them* effortlessly and without delay, *in* a single *instant*.

The second is:

> May whatever infinite superior merit has been gained
> In wholly dedicating this excellent conduct prayer,
> Cause migrators drowning in the river of
>   unsatisfactoriness
> To utterly gain the place of Amitābha.

Whatever infinite superior merits and good qualities ***have been gained*** by having recited ***this excellent conduct prayer***, contemplated its meanings, and trained in its conducts have been ***wholly dedicated*** to gaining the rank of an unsurpassed complete buddha. These infinite merits would not, as was explained earlier, be finished with even if expressed for aeons for they are merits ***infinite*** as space. Superior merit is merit connected with enlightenment, which is superior compared to all other types of merit.

What would those roots of virtue have been be dedicated to? Generally, they would have been dedicated for the sake of sentient beings, the ***migrators*** of the six classes, the ones who are ***drowning in the river of*** the great ***unsatisfactoriness*** of karma and affliction. Particularly, they would be dedicated to the ones who in the three bad migrations are scared and protectorless, suffering unbearably in the intense dungeons of the hot and cold hells, in the hunger and thirst of the pretas, and in the stupidity and thickness of the animals.

Thus, this infinite superior merit is dedicated so that they may be divorced from all the karmic appearances of the six classes of migrators together with their sufferings and latencies. It is also dedicated so that they are drawn up by Amitābha's hook of compassionate activity, born in his western field Sukhāvatī of complete purity, then complete the journey through the levels and paths until one day they gain the rank of unsurpassed complete buddhahood. In other words, it is dedicated ***to*** their ***utterly gaining the place of Amitābha***.

Coming after that verse, there is also the translator Vairochana's translation prayer:[106]

> The chief of these supreme prayers in this king of prayers,
> Brings benefit to all the infinite migrators;
> May this scripture adorned with Samantabhadra be accomplished
> And all the places of bad migrations be emptied.

The chief among the supreme results of these prayers of *A King of Prayers of Excellent Conduct* is the rank of unsurpassed complete buddhahood. Therefore, there is the vastness of reference, which is that all the sentient beings, the migrators infinite as space, are referenced without bias. And, there is the vastness of type, which is that all sentient beings pass successively through excellent births of gods and men, having good circumstances temporarily, and are made to gain the rank of complete buddha, the ultimate benefit. And there is the fact that this scripture is beautifully adorned with the profound and vast words of the prayer, the way to enter the ocean-like aspects of bodhisatva Noble Samantabhadra's enlightenment conduct. May the entirety of the meanings of prayers in this scripture be accomplished effortlessly, and, based on the fruitions of them, may all of the places without exception of the bad migrations of the fields of the ten directions be shaken out and emptied!

The colophon is: "*Noble One, a Prayer of Excellent Conduct* is complete".

---

[106] This verse is not part of the original prayer, as explained in the introduction to the book. The colophon is not part of the prayer either, but is part of the framework invented by Tibetans for their official translations of texts into the Tibetan language. The framework is mentioned in the introduction and fully described in my own commentary in volume I.

By the virtue of this effort here, may sentient beings equal to
    space,
And especially all migrators of the three bad migrations,
Utterly journey to the supreme field Sukhāvatī then
Manifest the fruition, unsurpassed complete enlightenment.

At the great dharma place Taklung Alpha Purity Elaboration-Free Sanctuary, the stupid one of no knowledge who wears a black hat, the one named Ontrul, wrote this during the winter time, thinking that it might be of benefit because of urging the householders, who like me are stupid idiots, to virtue. May it also be a cause for all infinite sentient beings to gain buddhahood.

Virtue! Virtue! Virtue!

GLOSSARY

Actuality, Tib. gnas lugs: A key term in both sutra and tantra and one of a pair of terms, the other being "apparent reality" (Tib. snang lugs). The two terms are used when determining the reality of a situation. The actuality of any given situation is how (lugs) the situation actuality sits or is present (gnas); the apparent reality is how (lugs) any given situation appears (snang) to an observer. Something could appear in many different ways, depending on the circumstances at the time and on the being perceiving it but, regardless of those circumstances, it will always have its own actuality of how it really is.

Affliction, Skt. kleśha, Tib. nyon mongs: This term is usually translated as emotion or disturbing emotion, etcetera, but the Buddha was very specific about the meaning of this word. When the Buddha referred to the emotions, meaning a movement of mind, he did not refer to them as such but called them "kleśha" in Sanskrit, meaning exactly "affliction". It is a basic part of the Buddhist teaching that emotions afflict beings, giving them problems at the time and causing more problems in the future.

Appearance and becoming, Tib. snang srid: This is a stock phrase meaning all of samsara (or sometimes all of samsara and nirvana). Appearance refers to the worlds and becoming refers to the sentient beings in those worlds whose existence is called "becoming". It is equivalent to another stock phrase "containers and contents" and the two are sometimes put together.

Arousing the mind, Tib. sems bskyed: This is general term used to mean the deliberate rousing of a particular mind. It is frequently used in the Great Vehicle to mean "arousing the enlightenment mind". The Great Vehicle path can be summed up as: arousing the mind of enlightenment, engaging in the conduct of enlightenment, and making prayers for enlightenment. This summary is readily apparent in the commentary in this book to Samantabhadra's Prayer. Note that there are two types of arousing the mind—fictional and superfactual; see under fictional enlightenment mind and superfactual enlightenment mind.

Authoritative statement, Skt.agama, Tib lung. Although often translated as "scripture", authentic statement means statement made by someone who has the true knowledge needed to make fully reliable statements about a subject. It is often used to indicate dharma taught by the Buddha or his disciples which is authoritative because of its source. It is also used in the pair "authoritative statement and realization" which, the Buddha explained, summed up the ways of transmitting his realization.

Becoming, Skt. bhāvanā, Tib. srid pa: This is another name for samsaric existence. Beings in samsara have a samsaric existence but, more than that, they are constantly in a state of becoming—becoming this type of being or that type of being in this abode or that, as they are driven along without choice by the karmic process that drives samsaric existence. It is sometimes used to mean any kind of existence, whether on the side of nirvana or samsara, for example in the phrase "appearance and becoming" explained earlier in the glossary and used in the commentary to Samantabhadra's Prayer.

Bliss, Skt. sukha, Tib. bde: The Sanskrit term and its Tibetan translation are usually translated as "bliss" but refer to the whole range of possibilities of everything on the side of good as opposed to bad. Thus, the term will mean pleasant, happy, good, nice, easy, comfortable, blissful, and so on, depending on context.

Bodhichitta, Tib. byang chub sems: See under enlightenment mind.

Bodhisatva, Tib. byang chub sems dpa': A bodhisatva is a person who has engendered the bodhichitta, enlightenment mind, and, with that as a basis, has undertaken the path to the enlightenment of a truly complete buddha specifically for the welfare of other beings.

Note that, despite the common appearance of "bodhisattva" in Western books on Buddhism, the Tibetan tradition has steadfastly maintained since the time of the earliest translations that the correct spelling is bodhisatva; see under satva and sattva.

Capable One, Skt. muni, Tib. thub pa: The term "muni" as for example in "Shakyamuni" has long been thought to mean "sage" because of an entry in Monier-Williams excellent Sanskrit-English dictionary. In fact, it has been used by many Indian religions since the times of ancient India to mean in general, a religious practitioner "one who could do it", one who has made progress on a spiritual path and thereby become able to restrain his three doors away from non-virtue and affliction.

Clinging, Tib. zhen pa: In Buddhism, this term refers specifically to the twofold process of dualistic mind mis-taking things that are not true, not pure, as true, pure, etcetera and then, because of seeing them as highly desirable even though they are not, attaching itself to or clinging to those things. This type of clinging acts as a kind of glue that keeps a person joined to the unsatisfactory things of cyclic existence because of mistakenly seeing them as desirable.

Compassionate activity, Tib. thugs rje: This does not mean compassionate activity in general. Rather, it is a specific term of the most profound level of teachings of Mahāmudrā and Great Completion, though it is sometimes seen in Great Vehicle texts, for example in the commentary here to Samantabhadra's Prayer. It is the quality of wisdom which choicelessly, ceaselessly, spontaneously, and pervasively acts to benefit others.

Complete purity, rnam dag: This term refers to a buddha's situation given that a buddha is completely free of the impurity of samsara.

Containers and contents, Tib. snod bcud: Containers are the outer worlds and environment and their contents are the beings living in them. This phrase is sometimes extended to "outer and inner, containers and contents" with the same meaning. It usually means "the entirety of samsara", though sometimes means "the entirety of samsara and nirvana".

Cyclic existence: See under samsara.

Dharmadhatu, Skt. dharmadhātu, Tib. chos kyi dbyings: This is the name for the *dhātu* meaning range or basic space in which all *dharma*s, meaning all phenomena, come into being. If a flower bed is the place where flowers grow and are found, the dharmadhātu is the dharma or phenomena bed in which all phenomena come into being and are found.

Dharmakaya, Skt. dharmakāya, Tib. chos sku: In the general teachings of Buddhism, this refers to the mind of a buddha, with "dharma" meaning reality and "kāya" meaning body.

Dharmata, Skt. dharmatā, Tib. chos nyid: This is a general term meaning the way that something is, and can be applied to anything at all; it is similar in meaning to "actuality" *q.v.* For example, the dharmatā of water is wetness and the dharmatā of the becoming bardo is a place where beings are in a samsaric, or becoming mode, prior to entering a nature bardo. It is used frequently in Tibetan Buddhism to mean "the dharmatā of reality".

Dhyana, Skt. dhyāna, Tib. bsam gtan: A Sanskrit term technically meaning all types of mental absorption. Mental absorptions cultivated in the human realm generally result in births in the form realms which are deep forms of concentration in themselves. The practices of mental absorption done in the human realm and the godly existences of the form realm that result from them both are named "dhyāna". The term also means meditation in general where one is concentrating on something as a way of developing oneself spiritually.

Elaboration, Tib. spro ba: This is a general name for what is given off by dualistic mind as it goes about its conceptual business. The term is pejorative in that it implies that a story has been made up, unnecessarily, about something which is actually nothing, which is empty. Elaborations, because of what they are, prevent a person from seeing emptiness directly.

Endurance World, Tib. mi mjed 'jig rten: The Buddha named our planet and its cosmic zone "Endurance World" because the humans inhabiting the planet endure suffering. He also called it Endurance Field meaning the entire cosmic field within which our planet exists.

Enlightenment mind, Skt. bodhichitta, Tib. byang chub sems: This is a key term of the Great Vehicle. It is the type of mind that is connected not with the lesser enlightenment of an arhat but the enlightenment of a truly complete buddha. As such, it is a mind which is connected with the aim of bringing all sentient beings to that same level of buddhahood. A person who has this mind has entered the Great Vehicle and is either a bodhisatva or a buddha.

It is important to understand that "enlightenment mind" is used to refer equally to the minds of all levels of bodhisatva on the path to buddhahood and to the mind of a buddha who has completed the path. Therefore, it is not "mind striving for enlightenment" as is so often translated, but "enlightenment mind", meaning that kind of mind which is connected with the full enlightenment of a truly complete buddha and which is present in all those who belong to the Great Vehicle.

Evil, evil deed, Skt. papaṃ, Tib. sdig pa: The original Sanskrit means something which someone has done which is truly bad, rotten. Anyone who has done such a thing is looked down upon. The Tibetan for it relates to the idea of a scorpion, a nasty creature that will sting you and injure you. In Buddhism, the term does not have the Christian sense of evil but simply means action done that, being done under the influence of an affliction, degrades you now in other's eyes, degrades you now because of the bad karmic seeds that you have planted by doing it, and degrades you in the future because of the ripening of the bad karmas into unpleasant results.

Excellent conduct, Skt. bhadracharya, Tib. bzang po spyod pa: This is a general term for all ways of behaviour which are seen as good, commendable, excellent. Each group of beings has their own idea of what constitutes excellent conduct. Therefore, this one term includes all types of conduct which are seen as good, both worldly and spiritual. Although that is understood in Buddhism, it is often used to indicate the excellent conduct of a bodhisatva in particular. In that latter case, it is excellent because it is the conduct by which one gains the goodness of enlightenment and in that case it is equivalent to the more specific term "enlightenment conduct" which refers only to the conduct of a bodhisatva done for the purpose of attaining enlightenment.

Fathom, fathomless, unfathomable, Tib. dpag pa, dpag tu med pa: "To fathom" means "to penetrate something fully by a probing or calculating type of dualistic mind. Fathomless and unfathomable mean that the thing being referred to is to large to be fully penetrated by that sort of mind.

Fictional, Skt. saṃvṛtti, Tib. kun rdzob: This term is paired with the term "superfactual" *q.v.* In the past, these terms have been translated as "relative" and "absolute" respectively, but those translations are nothing like the original terms. These terms are extremely important in the Buddhist teaching so it is very important that they be corrected, but more than that, if the actual meaning of these terms is not presented, then the teaching connected with them cannot be understood.

The Sanskrit term saṃvṛitti means a deliberate invention, a fiction, a hoax. It refers to the mind of ignorance which, because of being obscured and so not seeing suchness, is not true but a fiction. The things that appear to that ignorance are therefore fictional. Nonetheless, the beings who live in this ignorance believe that the things that appear to them through the filter of ignorance are true, are real. Therefore, these beings live in fictional truth.

Fictional and superfactual: Fictional and superfactual are our greatly improved translations for "relative" and "absolute" respectively. Briefly, the original Sanskrit word for fiction means a deliberately produced *fiction* and refers to the world projected by a mind controlled by ignorance. The original word for superfact means "that *superior fact* that appears on the surface of the mind of a noble one who has transcended samsara" and refers to reality seen as it actually is. Relative and absolute do not convey this meaning at all and, when they are used, the meaning being presented is simply lost.

Fictional truth, Skt. saṃvṛittisatya, Tib. kun rdzob bden pa: See under fictional.

Fictional truth enlightenment mind, Tib. kun rdzob bden pa'i byang chub sems: One of a pair of terms explained in the Great Vehicle; the other is Superfactual Truth Enlightenment Mind. See under fictional truth and superfactual truth for information about those terms. Enlightenment mind is defined as two types. The fictional type is the conventional type: it is explained as consisting of love and great compassion within the framework of an intention to obtain truly complete enlightenment for the sake of all sentient beings. The superfactual truth type is the ultimate type: it is explained as the enlightenment mind that is directly perceiving emptiness.

Field, Field realm, Tib. zhing, zhing khams: This term is often translated "buddha-field" though there is no "buddha" in the term. There are many different types of "fields" in both samsara and nirvana. Thus there are fields that belong to enlightenment and ones that belong to ignorance. Moreover, just as there are "realms" of samsara—desire, form, and formless—so there are realms of nirvana—the fields dharmakāya, saṃbhogakāya, and nirmāṇakāya and these are therefore called "field realms".

Five paths, Tib. lam lnga: In the Prajñāpāramitā teachings of the Great Vehicle, the Buddha explained the entire Buddhist journey as a set of five paths called the paths of accumulation, connection, seeing, cultivation, and no more training. The first four paths are part of journeying to enlightenment; the fifth path is that one has actually arrived and has no more training to undergo. There are a set of five paths that describe the journey of the Lesser Vehicle and a set of five paths that describe the journey of the Greater Vehicle. The names are the same in each case but the details of what is accomplished at each stage are different.

Foremost instruction, Skt. upadeśha, Tib. man ngag: There are several types of instruction mentioned in Buddhist literature: there is the general level of instruction which is the meaning contained in the words of the texts of the tradition; on a more personal and direct level there is oral instruction which has been passed down from teacher to student from the time of the buddha; and on the most profound level there are foremost instructions which are not only oral instructions provided by one's guru but are special, core instructions that come out of personal experience and which convey the teaching concisely and with the full weight of personal experience. Foremost instructions or upadeśha are crucial to the Vajra Vehicle because these are the special way of passing on the profound instructions needed for the student's realization.

Guardian, Skt. nātha, Tib. mgon po: This name is a respectful title reserved for the buddhas. It means that they both protect and nurture sentient beings who they oversee, like a child who, having no parents has been given or has found a guardian. It is often translated as "protector" but that correctly translates another Sanskrit term to start with and on top of that is insufficient because it does not include the aspect of nurturing. It is also given to other beings such as bodhisatvas who have a similar quality, for example, Guardian Nāgārjuna and Guardian Maitreya.

Great Vehicle, Skt. mahāyāna, Tib. theg pa chen po: The Buddha's teachings as a whole can be summed up into three vehicles where a vehicle is defined as that which can carry a person to a certain destination. The first vehicle, called the Lesser Vehicle, contains the teachings designed to get an individual moving on the spiritual path through showing the unsatisfactory state of cyclic existence and an emancipation from that. However, that path is only concerned with personal emancipation and fails to take account of all of the beings that there are in existence. There used to be eighteen schools of Lesser Vehicle in India but the only one surviving nowadays is the Theravāda of south-east Asia. The Greater Vehicle is a step up from that. The Buddha explained that it was great in comparison to the Lesser Vehicle for seven reasons. The first of those is that it is concerned with attaining the truly complete enlightenment of a truly complete buddha for the sake of every sentient being where the Lesser Vehicle is concerned only with a personal liberation that is not truly complete enlightenment and which is achieved only for the sake of that practitioner. The Great Vehicle has two divisions: a conventional form in which the path is taught in a logical, conventional way, and an unconventional form in which the path is taught in a very direct way. This latter vehicle is called the Vajra Vehicle because it takes the innermost, indestructible (vajra) fact of reality of one's own mind as the vehicle to enlightenment.

Intentional conduct, Tib. mos spyod: A name in the Great Vehicle for the path activities done at levels of both accumulation and connection. At this level, one is still intending to directly realize emptiness. Note that intention is the name of one of the fifty-one mental events. Thus this name implies that it is conduct still at the level of dualistic being, though it is a good mind because it intends to reach non-dualistic being. Also, by definition there is no real accomplishment until the path of seeing is reached, so there is no real accomplishment at the level of intentional conduct. Intentional conduct as non-accomplishment followed by the three paths which are levels of accomplishment is a general presentation contained in the common vehicle.

Kaya, Skt. kāya, Tib. sku: The Sanskrit term means a functional or coherent collection of parts, similar to the French "corps", and hence also comes to mean "a body". It is used in Tibetan Buddhist texts specifically to distinguish bodies belonging to the enlightened side from ones belonging to the samsaric side.

Enlightened being in Buddhism is said to be comprised of one or more kayas. It is most commonly explained to consist of one, two, three, four, or five kāyas, though it is pointed out that there are infinite aspects to enlightened being and therefore it can also be said to consist of an infinite number of kāyas. In fact, these descriptions of enlightened being consisting of one or more kāyas are given for the sake of understanding what is beyond conceptual understanding so should not be taken as absolute statements.

The most common description of enlightened being is that it is comprised of three kāyas: dharma, saṃbhoga, and nirmāṇakāyas. Briefly stated, the dharmakāya is the body of truth, the saṃbhogakāya is the body replete with the good qualities of enlightenment, and the nirmāṇakāya is the body manifested into the worlds of samsara and nirvana to benefit beings.

Dharmakāya refers to that aspect of enlightened being in which the being sees the truth for himself and, in doing so, fulfils his own needs for enlightenment. The dharmakāya is purely mind, without form. The remaining two bodies are summed up under the heading of rūpakāyas or form bodies manifested specifically to fulfil the needs of all un-enlightened beings. "Saṃbhogakāya" has been mostly translated as "body of enjoyment" or "body of rapture" but it is clearly stated in Buddhist texts on the subject that the name refers to a situation replete with what is useful, that is, to the fact that the saṃbhogakāya contains all of the good qualities of enlightenment as needed to benefit sentient beings. The saṃbhogakāya is extremely subtle and not accessible by most sentient beings; the nirmāṇakāya is a coarser manifestation which can reach sentient beings in many ways. Nirmāṇakāya should not be thought of as a physical body but as the capability to express enlightened being in whatever way is needed throughout all the different worlds of sentient beings. Thus, as much as it appears as a supreme buddha who shows the dharma to beings, it also appears as anything needed within sentient beings worlds to give them assistance.

Latency, Skt. vāsanā, Tib. bag chags: The original Sanskrit has the meaning exactly of "latency". The Tibetan term translates that inexactly with "something sitting there (Tib. chags) within the environment of mind (Tib. bag)". Although it has become popular to translate this term into English with "habitual pattern", that is not its meaning. The term refers to a karmic seed that has been imprinted on the mindstream and is present there as a latency, ready and waiting to come into manifestation.

Lay aside, Tib. bshags pa: This term is usually translated as "confession" but that is not the meaning. The term literally means to cut something away and remove it from oneself. In Buddhism, it is used in the context of ridding oneself of the karmic seeds sown by bad karmic actions.

Buddhism is a totally non-theistic religion, so it is very important to understand that one is not confessing wrongdoings to anyone, including oneself. There is no granting of absolution in this system. As the Buddha himself said, he has no ability to purify the karmic stains of sentient beings, he can only teach them how to do so. The practice that he taught for ridding oneself of karmic wrongdoings is the practice of realizing for oneself that they hold the seed of future suffering, rousing regret, and distancing oneself from them. In doing so, one lays them aside.

There is a longer phrase that indicates the full practice of laying aside. The Tibetan phrase "mthol zhing shags pa" literally means "admitting and laying aside". Note that "admitting" also does not entail confession; it refers to that fact that one first has to admit or acknowledge to oneself that one has done something wrong, karmically speaking, and that it will have undesirable consequences. Without this, one cannot effectively take the second step of distancing oneself from the actions. Therefore, it is explained that the process of "laying aside" has to be understood to include the practice of "admission" because, without that acknowledgement, the laying aside cannot be done.

Lesser Vehicle, Skt. hīnayāna, Tib. theg pa dman pa: See under Great Vehicle.

Mara, Skt. māra, Tib. bdud: The Sanskrit term is closely related to the word "death". Buddha spoke of four classes of extremely negative influences that have the capacity to drag a sentient being deep into samsara. They are the "maras" or "kiss of death": of having a samsaric set of five skandhas; of having afflictions; of death itself; and of the son of gods, which means being seduced and taken in totally by sensuality.

Migrator, Tib. 'gro ba: Migrator is one of several terms that were commonly used by the Buddha to mean "sentient being". It shows sentient beings from the perspective of their constantly being forced to go here and there from one rebirth to another by the power of karma. They are like flies caught in a jar, constantly buzzing back and forth. The term is often translated using "beings" which is another general term for sentient beings but doing so loses the meaning entirely: Buddhist authors who know the tradition do not use the word loosely but use it specifically to give the sense of beings who are constantly and helplessly going from one birth to another, and that is how the term should be read.

Mind, Skt. chitta, Tib. sems: There are several terms for mind in the Buddhist tradition, each with its own, specific meaning. This term is the most general term for the samsaric type of mind. It refers to the type of mind that is produced because of fundamental ignorance of enlightened mind. Whereas the wisdom of enlightened mind lacks all complexity and knows in a non-dualistic way, this mind of un-enlightenment is a very complicated apparatus that only ever knows in a dualistic way.

Noble one, Skt. ārya, Tib. 'phags pa: In Buddhism, a noble one is a being who has become spiritually advanced to the point that he has passed beyond cyclic existence. According to the Buddha, the beings in cyclic existence were ordinary beings, spiritual commoners, and the beings who had passed beyond it were special, the nobility.

Ones Gone to Bliss: see under sugata.

Outflow, Skt. āsrāva, Tib. zag pa: The Sanskrit term means a bad discharge, like pus coming out of a wound. Outflows occur when wisdom loses its footing and falls into the elaborations of dualistic mind. Therefore, anything with duality also has outflows. This is sometimes translated as "defiled" or "conditioned" but these fail to capture the meaning. The idea is that wisdom can remain self-contained in its own unique sphere but, when it loses its ability to stay within itself, it starts to have leakages into dualism that are defilements on the wisdom. See also under un-outflowed.

Poisons, Tib. dug: In Buddhism, poison is a general term for the afflictions. For samsaric beings, the afflictions are poisonous things which harm them. The Buddha most commonly spoke of the three poisons, which are the principal afflictions of desire, aggression, and ignorance. He also spoke of "the five poisons" which is a slightly longer enumeration of the principal afflictions: desire, aggression, delusion, pride, and jealousy.

Prajna, Skt. prajñā, Tib. shes rab: The Sanskrit term, literally meaning "best type of mind" is defined as that which makes correct distinctions between this and that and hence which arrives at correct understanding. It has been translated as "wisdom" but that is not correct because it is, generally speaking, a mental event belonging to dualistic mind where "wisdom" is used to refer to the non-dualistic knower of a buddha. Moreover, the main feature of prajñā is its ability to distinguish correctly between one thing and another and hence to arrive at a correct understanding.

Rational mind, Tib. blo: Rational mind is one of several terms for mind in Buddhist terminology. It specifically refers to a mind that judges this against that. With rare exception it is used to refer to samsaric mind, given that samsaric mind only works in the dualistic mode of comparing this versus that. Because of this, the term is mostly used in a pejorative sense to point out samsaric mind as opposed to an enlightened type of mind.

This term has been commonly translated simply as "mind" but that fails to identify this term properly and leaves it confused with the many other words that are also translated simply as "mind". It is not just another mind but is specifically the sort of mind that creates the situation of this and that (*ratio* in Latin) and hence, at least in the teachings of Kagyu and Nyingma, upholds the duality of samsara. In that case, it is the very opposite of the essence of mind. Thus, this is a key term which should be noted and not just glossed over as "mind".

Realization, Tib. rtogs pa: Realization has a very specific meaning: it refers to correct knowledge that has been gained in such a way that the knowledge does not abate. There are two important points here. Firstly, realization is not absolute. It refers to the removal of obscurations, one at a time. Each time that a practitioner removes an obscuration, he gains a realization because of it. Therefore, there are as many levels of realization as there are obscurations. Maitreya, in the *Ornament of Manifest Realizations*, shows how the removal of the various obscurations that go with each of the three realms of samsaric existence produces realization. Secondly, realization is stable or, as the Tibetan wording says, "unchanging". As Guru Rinpoche pointed out, "Intellectual knowledge is like a patch, it drops away; experiences on the path are temporary, they evaporate like mist; realization is unchanging".

Reference and Referencing, Tib. dmigs pa: Referencing is the name for the process in which dualistic mind references an actual object by using a conceptual token instead of the actual object. Whatever is referenced is then called a reference. Note that these terms imply the presence of dualistic mind and their opposites, non-referencing and being without reference imply the presence of non-dualistic wisdom.

Refuge, Skt. śharaṇaṃ, Tib. bskyab pa: The Sanskrit term means "shelter", "protection from harm". Everyone seeks a refuge from the unsatisfactoriness of life, even if it is a simple act like brushing the teeth to prevent the body from decaying un-necessarily. Buddhists, after having thought carefully about their situation and who could provide a refuge from it which would be thoroughly reliable, find that three things—buddha, dharma, and sangha—are the only things that could provide that kind of refuge. Therefore, Buddhists take refuge in those Three Jewels of Refuge as they are called. Taking refuge in the Three Jewels is clearly laid out as the one doorway to all Buddhist practice and realization.

Samsara, Skt. saṃsāra, Tib. 'khor ba: This is the most general name for the type of existence in which sentient beings live. It refers to the fact that they continue on from one existence to another, always within the enclosure of births that are produced by ignorance and experienced as unsatisfactory. The original Sanskrit means to be constantly going about, here and there. The Tibetan term literally means "cycling", because of which it is frequently translated into English with "cyclic existence" though that is not quite the meaning of the term.

Satva and sattva: According to the Tibetan tradition established at the time of the great translation work done at Samye under the watch of Padmasambhava not to mention the one hundred and sixty-three of the greatest Buddhist scholars of Sanskrit-speaking India, there is a difference of meaning between the Sanskrit terms "satva" and "sattva", with satva meaning "an heroic kind of being" and "sattva" meaning simply "a being". According to the Tibetan tradition established under the advice of the Indian scholars mentioned above, satva is correct for the words Vajrasatva and bodhisatva, whereas sattva is correct for the words samayasattva, samādhisattva, and jñānasattva, and is also used alone to refer to any or all of these three sattvas.

All Tibetan texts produced since the time of the great translations conform to this system and all Tibetan experts agree that this is correct, but Western translators of Tibetan texts have for last few hundreds of years claimed that they know better and have "satva" to "sattva" in every case, causing confusion amongst Westerners confronted by the correct spellings. Recently, publications by Western Sanskrit scholars have been appearing in which these great experts finally admit that they were wrong and that the Tibetan system is and always has been correct!

Secrets (of a buddha): See under three secrets.

Shine forth, shining forth, Tib. shar ba: This term means "to dawn" or "to come forth into visibility" either in the outer physical world or in the inner world of mind.

It is heavily used in texts on meditation to indicate the process of something coming forth into mind. There are other terms with this specific meaning but most of them also imply the process of dawning within a samsaric mind. "Shine forth" is special because it does not have that restricted meaning; it refers to the process of something dawning in any type of mind, un-enlightened and enlightened.

Special intention, Tib. lhag bsam: This term is used in general to refer to all specially pure intentions. In Great Vehicle literature it will more often refer specifically to bodhichitta but even then, it can be used to mean bodhichitta in general or an especially pure instance of bodhichitta.

Sugata, Tib. bde bar gshegs pa: This term is one of many names for a buddha. It has the twofold meaning of someone who has gone on a good, pleasant, easy journey and who has arrived at a place which is good, pleasant, and full of ease. The meaning in relation to buddhahood is explained at length in *Unending Auspiciousness, the Sutra of the Recollection of the Noble Three Jewels* by Tony Duff, published by Padma Karpo Translation Committee, 2010, ISBN: 978-9937-8386-1-0.

Superfactual, Skt. paramārtha, Tib. don dam: This term is paired with the term "fictional" *q.v.* In the past, the terms have been translated as "relative" and "absolute" respectively, but those translations are nothing like the original terms. These terms are extremely important in the Buddhist teaching so it is very important that their translations be corrected but, more than that, if the actual meaning of these terms is not presented, the teaching connected with them cannot be understood.

The Sanskrit term literally means "the fact for that which is above all others, special, superior" and refers to the wisdom mind possessed by those who have developed themselves spiritually to the point of having transcended samsara. That wisdom is *superior* to an ordinary, un-developed person's consciousness and the *facts* that appear on its surface are superior compared to the facts that appear on the ordinary person's consciousness. Therefore, it is superfact or the holy fact, more literally. What this wisdom knows is true for the beings who have it, therefore what the wisdom sees is superfactual truth.

Superfactual truth, Skt. paramārthasatya, Tib. don dam bden pa: See under superfactual.

Superfactual truth enlightenment mind, Tib. don dam bden pa'i byang chub sems: This is one of a pair of terms; the other is Fictional Truth Enlightenment Mind *q.v.* for explanation.

Superfice, superficies, Tib. rnam pa: In discussions of mind, a distinction is made between the entity of mind which is a mere knower and the superficial things that appear on its surface and which are known by it. In other words, the superficies are the various things which pass over the surface of mind but which are not mind. Superficies are all the specifics that constitute appearance—for example, the colour white within a moment of visual consciousness, the sound heard within an ear consciousness, and so on.

Third order thousandfold world system, Tib. stong gsum 'jig rten: Indian cosmology has for its smallest cosmic unit a single Mt. Meru with four continents type of world system; an analogy might be a single planetary system like our solar system. One thousand of those makes a first order thousandfold world system; an analogy might be a galaxy. One thousand of those makes a second order thousandfold world system; an analogy might be a region of space with many galaxies. One thousand of those makes a third order thousandfold world system (1000 raised to the power 3); an analogy would be one whole universe like ours. The Buddha said that there were countless numbers of third order thousandfold world systems, each of which would be roughly equivalent to a universe like ours.

Three kayas: See under kaya.

Three secrets, Tib. gsang ba: This term is usually defined as a path term which refers to the body, speech, and mind of a person who is on the way to buddhahood. When a person becomes a buddha, he has reached his full state of enlightenment in which case the three secrets are referred to as the three vajras of a tathāgata because they are unchanging at that point. This path term is used to mean the three vajras of the fruition state of buddhahood.

Three Vehicles, theg pa gsum: The entire teachings of the Buddha can be summed up into three "vehicles". Each vehicle is a complete set of teachings that will take a person to a particular level of spiritual attainment. The first one, the Lesser Vehicle, is a set of teachings that will take a person out of cyclic existence but will not lead the person to full enlightenment. The second one, the Great Vehicle, is "great" relative to the Lesser Vehicle because it can lead a person to full enlightenment. The third vehicle, the Vajra Vehicle, also can lead a person to full enlightenment. The difference between the Great and Vajra Vehicles is that the first are exoteric teachings that are suitable for anyone whereas the second are esoteric teachings which are not. The Great Vehicle and the Vajra Vehicle both lead to the same attainment, but the first proceeds very gradually whereas the second is very fast. The Great Vehicle proceeds using the sutra teachings of the Buddha whereas the Vajra Vehicle proceeds using the tantric teachings.

The Translated Treatises, Tib. bstan 'gyur or Tangyur: This is the name of the collection of the official translations into the Tibetan language of the treatises of Buddhist masters that were made to support and clarify the meaning of the Buddha-word. These treatises are mainly those of Indian Buddhist masters but also include some by masters of other countries. The commentaries on Samantabhadra's Prayer preserved in the *Translated Treatises* are ones that were composed in the Sanskrit language by Indian masters and translated into Tibetan at the time of the great translations in Tibet.

The Translated Word, Tib. bka' 'gyur: This is the name of the collection of the official translations into the Tibetan language of the Buddha-word and words of great Buddhist masters in the time of the Buddha. There are seven major editions of *The Translated Word* in Tibetan. When doing this work, I used a recently produced version of the Derge edition which has all differences between it and the remaining six major editions carefully noted.

Tirthika, Skt. tīrthika, Tib. mu stegs pa: This is very kind name adopted by the Buddha for those who did not follow him but who, because they followed some other spiritual path, had at least started on the path back to enlightenment. The Sanskrit name means "those who have arrived at the steps at the edge of the pool". A lengthy explanation is given in the *Illuminator Tibetan-English Dictionary* by Tony Duff and published by Padma Karpo Translation Committee.

Un-outflowed, Skt. anāshrāva, Tib. zag pa med pa: Un-outflowed dharmas are ones that are connected with wisdom that has not lost its footing and leaked out into a defiled state; it is self-contained wisdom without any taint of dualistic mind and its apparatus. See also out flowed.

Unsatisfactoriness, Skt. duḥkha, Tib. sdug bngal: This term is usually translated into English with "suffering" but there are many problems with that. When the Buddha talked about the nature of samsaric existence, he said that it was unsatisfactory. He used the term "duḥkha", which includes actual suffering but means much more than that. Duḥkha is one of a pair of terms, the other being "sukha", which is usually translated as, but does not only mean, bliss. The real meaning of duḥkha is "everything on the side of bad"—not good, uncomfortable, unpleasant, not nice, and so on. Thus, it means "unsatisfactory in every possible way". The real meaning of its opposite, sukha, is "everything on the side of good"—not bad, comfortable, pleasant, nice, and so on. Therefore, that he is completely liberated from the sufferings actually means that he has completely liberated himself from the unsatisfactoriness of samsara, which includes all types of suffering and happiness, too.

Wisdom, Skt. jñāna, Tib. ye shes: This is a fruition term that refers to the kind of mind, the kind of knower possessed by a buddha. Sentient beings do have this kind of knower but it is covered over by a very complex apparatus for knowing, dualistic mind. If they practise the path to buddhahood, they will leave behind their obscuration and return to having this kind of knower.

The Sanskrit term has the sense of knowing in the most simple and immediate way. This sort of knowing is present at the core of every being's mind. Therefore, the Tibetans called it "the particular type of awareness which is there primordially". Because of the Tibetan wording it has often been called "primordial wisdom" in English translations, but that goes too far; it is just "wisdom" in the sense of the most fundamental knowing possible.

About the Author, Padma Karpo Translation Committee, And Their Supports for Study

I have been encouraged over the years by all of my teachers to pass on the knowledge I have accumulated in a lifetime dedicated to study and practice, primarily in the Tibetan tradition of Buddhism. On the one hand, they have encouraged me to teach. On the other, they are concerned that, while many general books on Buddhism have been and are being published, there are few books that present the actual texts of the tradition. Therefore they, together with a number of major figures in the Buddhist book publishing world, have also encouraged me to translate and publish high quality translations of individual texts of the tradition.

My teachers always remark with great appreciation on the extraordinary amount of teaching that I have heard in this life. It allows for highly informed, accurate translations of a sort not usually seen. Briefly, I spent the 1970's studying, practising, then teaching the Gelugpa system at Chenrezig Institute, Australia, where I was a founding member and also the first Australian to be ordained as a monk in the Tibetan Buddhist tradition. In 1980, I moved to the United States to study at the feet of the Vidyadhara Chogyam Trungpa Rinpoche. I stayed in his Vajradhatu community, now called Shambhala, where I studied and practised all the Karma Kagyu, Nyingma, and Shambhala teachings being presented there and was a senior member of the Nalanda Translation Committee. After the vidyadhara's nirvana, I moved in 1992 to Nepal, where I have been continuously involved with the study, practise, translation, and teaching of the Kagyu system and especially of the Nyingma system of Great Completion. In recent years, I have spent extended times in Tibet with the greatest living Tibetan masters of Great Completion, receiving very pure transmissions of the ultimate levels of this teaching directly in Tibetan and practising them there in retreat. In that way, I have studied and practised extensively not in one Tibetan tradition as is usually done, but in three of the four Tibetan traditions—Gelug, Kagyu, and Nyingma—and also in the Theravada tradition, too.

With that as a basis, I have taken a comprehensive and long term approach to the work of translation. For any language, one first must have the lettering needed to write the language. Therefore, as a member of the Nalanda Translation Committee, I spent some years in the 1980's making Tibetan word-processing software and high-quality Tibetan fonts. After that, reliable lexical works are needed. Therefore, during the 1990's I spent some years writing the *Illuminator Tibetan-English Dictionary* and a set of treatises on Tibetan grammar, preparing a variety of key Tibetan reference works needed for the study and translation of Tibetan Buddhist texts, and giving our Tibetan software the tools needed to translate and research Tibetan texts. During this time, I also translated full-time for various Tibetan gurus and ran the Drukpa Kagyu Heritage Project—at the time the largest project in Asia for the preservation of Tibetan Buddhist texts. With the dictionaries, grammar texts, and specialized software in place, and a wealth of knowledge, I turned my attention in the year 2000 to the translation and publication of important texts of Tibetan Buddhist literature.

Padma Karpo Translation Committee (PKTC) was set up to provide a home for the translation and publication work. The committee focusses on producing books containing the best of Tibetan literature, and, especially, books that meet the needs of practitioners. At the time of writing, PKTC has published a wide range of books that, collectively, make a complete program of study for those practising

Tibetan Buddhism, and especially for those interested in the higher tantras. All in all, you will find many books both free and for sale on the PKTC web-site. Most are available both as paper editions and e-books.

It would take up too much space here to present an extensive guide to our books and how they can be used as the basis for a study program. However, a guide of that sort is available on the PKTC web-site, whose address is on the copyright page of this book and we recommend that you read it to see how this book fits into the overall scheme of PKTC publications. Other sutra publications of interest would be:

- *Unending Auspiciousness, the Sutra of the Recollection of the Noble Three Jewels* by Tony Duff, published by Padma Karpo Translation Committee, 2010, ISBN: 978-9937-838-61-0.
- *Maitreya's Sutras and Prayer, with Commentary by Padma Karpo*, by Tony Duff, published by Padma Karpo Translation Committee, February 2013, ISBN 978-9937-572-62-0. The book presents two sutras petitioned by Maitreya and his famous prayer, and a commentary to the prayer by Padma Karpo.
- *The Noble One Called "Point of Passage Wisdom", A Great Vehicle Sutra*, t by Tony Duff, published by Padma Karpo Translation Committee, 2010, ISBN: 978-9937-572-58-3. The root sutra of the ten profound essence sutras of Other Emptiness of the third turning of the wheel.
- *Sutra of the Householder Uncouth, A Teaching of the Buddha Showing All-knowing Wisdom And the Householder's Way*, by Tony Duff and Tamás Agócs, published by Padma Karpo Translation Committee, 2013, ISBN 978-9937-572-56-9.
- *Samantabhadra's Prayer Volume I, with commentaries by Nāgārjuna and Tony Duff.*

We make a point of including, where possible, the relevant Tibetan texts in Tibetan script in our books. We also make them available in electronic editions that can be downloaded free from our website, as discussed below. The Tibetan texts for this book were too large to include, so they have been made available in digital format for download on the PKTC web-site.

Electronic Resources

PKTC has developed a complete range of electronic tools to facilitate the study and translation of Tibetan texts. For many years now, this software has been a prime resource for Tibetan Buddhist centres throughout the world, including in Tibet itself. It is available through the PKTC web-site.

The wordprocessor TibetDoc has the only complete set of tools for creating, correcting, and formatting Tibetan text according to the norms of the Tibetan language. It can also be used to make texts with mixed Tibetan and English or other languages. Extremely high quality Tibetan fonts, based on the forms of Tibetan calligraphy learned from old masters from pre-Communist Chinese Tibet, are also available. Because of their excellence, these typefaces have achieved a legendary status amongst Tibetans.

TibetDoc is used to prepare electronic editions of Tibetan texts in the PKTC text input office in Asia. Tibetan texts are often corrupt so the input texts are carefully corrected prior to distribution. After that, they are made available through the PKTC web-site. These electronic texts are not careless productions like so many of the Tibetan texts found on the web, but are highly reliable editions useful to non-scholars and scholars alike. Some of the larger collections of these texts are for purchase, but most are available for free download.

The electronic texts can be read, searched, and even made into an electronic library using either TibetDoc or our other software, TibetD Reader. Like TibetDoc, TibetD Reader is advanced software with many capabilities made specifically to meet the needs of reading and researching Tibetan texts. PKTC software is for purchase but we make a free version of TibetD Reader available for free download on the PKTC web-site.

A key feature of TibetDoc and Tibet Reader is that Tibetan terms in texts can be looked up on the spot using PKTC's electronic dictionaries. PKTC also has several electronic dictionaries—some Tibetan-Tibetan and some Tibetan-English—and a number of other reference works. The *Illuminator Tibetan-English Dictionary* is renowned for its completeness and accuracy.

This combination of software, texts, reference works, and dictionaries that work together seamlessly has become famous over the years. It has been the basis of many, large publishing projects within the Tibetan Buddhist community around the world for over thirty years and is popular amongst all those needing to work with Tibetan language or deepen their understanding of Buddhism through Tibetan texts.

INDEX

A King of Prayers of Excellent
   Conduct 35, 38, 155
a prayer of excellent conduct   155
abandoned bad companions . 30,
          140
Abhidharma 51, 53
accomplishment of great prayers
   55
accumulation of merit 116
activities 60, 82, 87, 127, 164
actuality . . . 62, 64, 66, 117, 129,
      131, 144, 148, 157
admiring 23, 58, 60, 84, 115
admiring, longing, and trusting
   60
Adzom Gyalsay . . . . . xxi, 55, 74
Adzom Gyalsay's commentary
   . . . . 59, 67, 85
affliction 26, 29, 30, 91, 105,
   129-131, 137, 138, 154, 157, 159,
               161
Amitābha . . . . xi, 30-32, 89, 102,
      112, 140, 141, 150-152, 154
an ocean of wisdom   29, 130, 131
antidote . . . 47, 77, 80, 105, 129,
         130, 138, 143
appearance and becoming 92, 157
appearance of interdependency 64
appearances of impurity 65
appearances of interdependency
   64
appearances of purity 65
armour 46, 88, 109, 110
armour of courage 110
arousing the mind . . . 74, 86, 92,
          128, 158
atoms of the fields . . 30, 62, 139
authoritative statement 158
authoritative statements 113
Avabhraṃsha 49
Avataṃsaka Sutra . . . . xiii, 55, 74
bad companions 30, 140
bad migrations 6, 26, 30, 35,
   85, 94, 103, 108, 109, 124, 140,
   154-156
bardo 160
beautiful fine lotus 32, 151
become buddhas at the stage
   . . . . 28, 126
become ordained 26, 96, 97
becoming .. xxviii, 12, 17, 23, 29,
   53, 73, 91-93, 97, 121, 132, 147,
   157, 158, 160
benefit and ease .. 25, 46, 84, 85,

88, 108, 128, 142, 147
beyond-ordinary levels of
  experience xiv
Bhadravaha .... xvi, 54
bhikṣhu 78, 79, 95, 112, 125, 131, 141, 143
bit-wise commentary xx
bliss 24, 53, 66, 67, 158, 168, 174
bodhi tree 25, 31, 90-92, 146, 147
bodhichitta 158, 161, 171
bodhisattva .... x, 159
bodhisatva ..... iv, v, x-xiv, xxiv, xxvii, 1, 3-17, 21-23, 32, 38, 47, 48, 50-52, 54-57, 59, 61, 63, 64, 66, 67, 69, 73, 76, 79, 80, 82, 84-86, 89, 92, 94, 97, 98, 100, 107, 108, 110, 114, 116-119, 122, 123, 125-129, 131, 133-137, 139-142, 146, 148-151, 155, 158, 159, 161, 164, 170
bodhisatva level .. x, xiv, xxiv, 52, 97, 125, 151
bodhisatva levels . 23, 54, 55, 94, 123, 126
bodhisatva mahāsatva 5, 7, 8, 17, 23, 38
bodhisatva mahāsatva
  Samantabhadra . 5, 7, 8, 17, 23, 38
bodhisatva sons .. x, xi, 9, 63, 92, 119
bodhisatva's conduct x-xii, 51, 80
boundless universes of field
  realms 60
Brahma's speech 66
branches of sound 28, 120
breadth of merely a hair . 27, 118
buddha sons .. 24, 25, 27, 62, 63, 80, 90, 92, 118, 119

buddha speech . 28, 47, 120, 121
buddhas at the enlightenment
  stage 25, 82
buddhas at the stage 28, 126
buddha-fields 4-6, 9-23, 38, 118, 125, 134
buddha's purification of a field 92
bundle 3
Capable One 61, 159
Chandrakīrti 67
Changkya Rolpa'i Dorje .... xix, 54, 121, 122, 126
chief of the sons 29, 133
chief of the sons of all the
  conquerors 29, 133
clinging ... 5, 99, 128, 130, 159
colophon 155
commendation ... 10, 24, 66, 67
commentaries on the prayer . iii, xvii-xix
*Commentary on the Meaning of
  Enlightenment Mind* 103
compassionate activity .. 62, 109, 115, 154, 159
complete emancipation . 4, 5, 17, 28, 117, 122, 124
complete emancipations . 23, 27, 116-118
complete purity . 5, 6, 11, 21, 23, 28, 99, 120, 134, 154, 159
completing, ripening, and
  cleansing
  explanation 61
completing, ripening, and
  purifying 61, 130, 133
complexion 145
conclusion .... xiii, xx, 88
conduct of a bodhisatva .... v, x-xiii, 107, 161
conduct of enlightenment ... 75,

INDEX 183

90, 101, 150, 158
conducts of enlightenment .. 26, 94, 110
confession 166
conquerors 24-31, 53, 60-63, 66-68, 70-75, 77, 80, 90-92, 98, 111, 114, 115, 120, 121, 123, 125, 132, 133, 138, 139, 144, 149
containers and contents 125, 134, 159
critical edition of the prayer xxiii
cyclic existence ..... xi, 159, 164, 167, 172
death transfers and births 26, 96
dedication of merit xi
descend to buddhahood 25, 89, 90
dharmadhātu 5, 9, 14, 56, 63, 160
dharmadhātus ... 4, 7, 8, 10-12, 24, 62
dharmakāya . 115, 128, 151, 160, 163, 165
dharmatā 62, 63, 65, 86, 109, 160
dhyāna 160
diacritical marks .... ii, xxviii
Dignāga .... xvi, 54
direct perception . 15, 24, 27, 31, 56, 60, 61, 64, 114, 118, 119, 124, 125, 131, 140, 141, 150
discipline conduct 26, 98
discipline type of conduct ... 98
divisions of the actual prayer
.... 46, 88
divisions of the prayer 137
domains 28, 120, 124
downfall 78, 80
Dromtonpa 111
Dza Patrul ..... xxi, 50, 85, 137
Dzogchen .. iii, xii, xx, xxi, 51, 55, 109
Dzogchen Monastery ... xxi, 55

Dzogchen Patrul 55
Eastern Tibet xxi
eight complete emancipations 117
eighteen unmixed ones 60, 67, 123
elaboration 42, 124, 156, 160
emancipation ... 4, 5, 17, 28, 76, 79, 96, 103, 113, 117, 122, 124, 129, 139, 141, 164
Emblic Myrobalan 82
emptiness ... 53, 64, 78, 86, 105, 107, 117, 149, 160, 163, 164, 177
end of every sentient 30, 137
end of karma and affliction .. 30, 137
end of space 30, 137
end of the prayer .... xii, 47, 137
Endurance World ... 13, 16, 59, 84, 160
English ..... iii, v-ix, xiii-xv, xix-xxvi, xxviii, xxix, 3, 49, 101, 145, 159, 166, 170, 173, 174, 176, 178, 179
English translation .... vi, viii, xx
enlightened conduct 135
enlightenment conduct .. 26, 27, 29, 50, 101, 109, 111, 115, 116, 118, 123, 126, 130-132, 135, 138, 155
compared to excellent conduct
.... 50
enlightenment mind . 17, 18, 26, 46, 51, 78, 86, 88, 93, 94, 97, 98, 102-105, 107, 110, 142, 145, 146, 158, 161-163, 172
entering .... x-xii, 22, 23, 27, 28, 47, 48, 52, 67, 88, 101, 110, 111, 116, 118-124, 135, 146, 148, 149, 160
entering into all future aeons

.... 28, 122
entering into intention and
   production 47, 124
entering into turning the dharma
   wheel 47, 121
Entering into viewing the
   tathāgatas 47
Entering the Bodhisatva's Conduct
.... x-xii
entering the buddha speech .. 47,
   120
Entering the Middle Way 52,
   67, 148
entering viewing the fields and
   buddhas 118
European languages .. viii, ix, xix,
   xxiv
evil .. 31, 45, 76-80, 87, 94, 103-
   105, 111, 140, 142-146, 150, 161
evil deeds . 31, 78, 103, 140, 142-
   145, 150
evil deeds of the five immediates
   .... 31, 142, 143
excellent conduct ... v, xi, xii, 24,
   26, 27, 29-32, 35, 38, 43, 50-52,
   54, 57, 60, 61, 73, 75, 94, 96,
   98, 111, 113, 115, 116, 129,
   130, 132, 134, 135, 139-151,
   153-155, 161
excellent conduct of a bodhisatva
   .... v, xi, xii, 161
excellent conduct of
   enlightenment 150
excellent conduct of the six
   pāramitās 51, 60
excellent conduct prayer . 24, 30-
   32, 50, 51, 54, 57, 60, 96, 140-
   144, 148, 153, 154
excellent dedications ... 29, 133
explanations of the prayer ... iii,
   vi-ix, xv
faith in supreme enlightenment
   .... 30, 139
fathomless .. 118, 120, 123, 132,
   140, 152, 162
fictional .. 73, 98, 117, 148, 158,
   162, 172
fictional and superfactual 98, 162
fictional enlightenment mind 158
fictional truth 148, 162, 172
fictional truth enlightenment
   mind 162, 172
field arrangements . 28, 124- 126
field arrangements of other
   buddhas 126
field atoms ... 24, 25, 60-63, 66,
   84, 85, 89, 115, 119, 122, 126
field realm 125, 152, 163
fields ... 4-6, 9-23, 25, 27-30, 38,
   47, 62, 69, 71, 83, 90, 91, 107-
   109, 114, 118, 119, 125, 126,
   130, 132-134, 138, 139, 155, 163
fifth buddha of this era x
final end of space 30, 137
finest clothes 24, 68
finest flowers 24, 68
finest garlands 24, 68
finest incense 24, 68
first to seventh bodhisatva levels
   126
first-level person 52
five important prayers ..... iii, x
five paths 82, 163
five silk garments 69, 71
five-coloured silks 71
force of loving kindnesses 28, 127
force of one's own faith and
   devotion 62
force of rational mind 28, 32, 121
force of rejection 77

force of the compassionate activity and blessings 62
forces . 24, 28, 29, 47, 60, 61, 73, 75, 77, 80, 88, 105, 109, 116, 127-131, 135, 141, 143
forces of affliction .. 29, 129, 130
forces of antidote 77, 143
forces of conduct ... 28, 127, 128
forces of enlightenment .. 29, 88, 127, 130
forces of excellent conduct .. 24, 29, 60, 129, 130
forces of excellent conduct prayer 24, 60
forces of faith 24, 73
forces of faith in excellent conduct 24, 73
forces of karma 29, 129
forces of māra 29, 129, 130
forces of merit 29, 127
forces of miracles 28, 127
forces of vehicle 28, 127
forces of wisdom 29, 127
foremost instructions 163
foundation of completely pure discipline 55
four forces of the antidote 77, 80
four non-fears .. 60, 67, 123, 128
framework .. vii, viii, xiv, xv, xviii, xxii, xxiv, xxvi, xxix, 155, 163
fully illuminating 27, 115
future lives 141
Gaṇḍavyūha Sutra .. iv, xiii, xvii, xxii, xxvi, 3, 35, 38
galaxies 172
Gelugpa .... xix, 175
gender issues .... iv, xxvii
general term 158, 160, 161, 167, 168
gods of the Heaven of the Thirty-Three 75
Going As A Hero Samādhi . 129
gone in the three times .. 28, 29, 31, 58, 123, 124, 132, 149
gone to suchness 59
good and pleasing maṇḍala .. 32, 151, 152
good qualities ... 4, 7, 19, 24, 27, 30, 59, 63, 66, 67, 74, 90, 97, 98, 100, 101, 116, 117, 122, 123, 129, 133, 136, 137, 142, 144, 145, 152, 154, 165
good qualities of all the conquerors 24, 66
grammar .... vi, xvi, xvii, xix, xxi, xxv, 58, 115, 176
great arousing of mind 50
great compassion ... 4, 9, 19, 23, 104, 128, 163
great enlightenment ... 139, 140
Great Mañjughosha 69
Great Vehicle ... iii, v, x, xii, xiii, xv, xvii, xxiii, xxv, 1, 3, 38, 51, 101, 152, 158, 159, 161-164, 167, 171-173, 177
guardian buddhas 83
guru ... xii, 19, 87, 106, 163, 169
hearing, contemplation, and meditation 112, 115, 120
Heaven of the Thirty-Three . 75
hell 13, 78, 95, 109, 142, 143
higher training of discipline . 98
higher training of prajñā 53
incense 10, 24, 68, 70-73
incense powders 71, 72
Indian commentaries .. iii, vi-viii, xvi-xviii, xxiii, xxiv, 51, 58, 67, 74, 75, 108, 119, 137
Indian experts xviii
Indian masters ... vi, xvi, xvii, xx,

intentional conduct ... xxiii, 136, 173
intentional conduct ... 164, 165
interdependency 64, 65, 80
intervening state 97
Jigmey Lingpa .... xxi, 107, 133
Jigmey Tennyi 96, 143
Jinamitra 32, 35, 38
Jowo Je 65, 102
Jowo Je Dīpaṃkāra 102
Kadampa Putowa 102
Kanakamuni 59, 89
karma and affliction 30, 131, 137, 138, 154
karma and afflictions .. 106, 116, 123, 131, 138
Karma Chagmey ...... xviii, 83
karma, affliction, and māra's works 26, 105
karmas of evil 87, 103
karmic lot 6
Kāshyapa 59, 89
Kaushika 75, 83
kāya ... 69, 71, 91, 92, 115, 116, 128, 145, 151, 153, 160, 163, 165, 166
key point of all dharmas being interdependent 64
king of prayers ... 35, 38, 49, 51, 139, 141, 155
Krakucchanda 59
lamps .. 7, 24, 25, 28, 68, 70, 73, 82, 126
lamps of the worlds 25, 82
language of the flesh-eating spirits 49
lay aside 166
laying aside ... 25, 45, 76-79, 85, 166, 167
laying aside evil 45, 76
leader of the gandharvas 54

leading bodhi tree 25, 31, 90, 146
Lesser Vehicle .. 51, 97, 98, 163, 164, 167, 172, 173
limb of dedicating 46, 85
limb of laying aside 45, 76
limb of making offerings . 45, 68
limb of prostration ... 45, 58, 75
limb of rejoicing 45, 80
limb of supplicating 46, 84
limb of urging 45, 82
line of the tathāgatas xxvii
lions of men 23, 28, 58, 60, 123, 124
literal meaning .. xv, xvii, 54, 137
Lochen .... xix, 54, 59, 114, 116, 120, 124
Lochen Dharmaśhrī . xix, 54, 114
Lodro Gyatso xxi
Longchen Nyingthig xxi
Longchen Rabjam 144
Lovely to Behold 69, 91, 144, 152
Mahāyāna .... x, 164
maṇḍala of the three kāyas ... 92
Maitreya .... x, xi, 50, 59, 90, 99, 164, 169, 177
Maitreya the Guardian 59
Maitreya's Prayer ... x, xi, 50, 99
Mañjughoṣha 47, 69
Mañjuśhrī .. x, 30, 31, 35, 48, 50, 53, 134, 135, 148, 149
Mañjuśhrī's Prayer x
māra 26, 29, 31, 62, 91, 92, 105, 106, 123, 129, 130, 145, 147, 152, 167
māra's works 26, 105
Maudgyalyāyana 112
Maudgyalyāyana and Śhāripūtra 112
meaning of the title .. 45, 49, 51
meeting the view 62

men and women . xx, xxvii, 43, 61
metaphor 18, 56, 141
methods 73, 102, 128
migrator sentient beings . 93, 97, 114, 120, 137
migrators .. 4, 20, 25, 26, 32, 35, 61, 80, 84, 85, 92, 93, 97, 105, 107-109, 116, 120, 128, 133, 134, 138, 151, 154-156
mind for supreme enlightenment 60, 74, 75
Mindroling monastery xix
Mipham 65
miracle 150
miracles 14, 28, 66, 73, 112, 123-127, 137, 142, 151, 152
miraculous birth 151
misunderstandings of Sanskrit syntax xxiv
mixed incense powders 72
mixed powders equal to Mt. Meru 24, 68
mode of phenomena 65
modes of the wheel 28, 121
Mt. Meru . 13, 24, 68, 72, 81, 172
Muni ... x, xi, 59, 63, 68, 71, 89, 91, 95, 110, 112, 147, 148, 159
my own commentary ... xxvi, 59, 67, 82, 90, 96, 126, 155
Nāgārjuna .... iv, xvi-xviii, xxiii, xxvi, 52, 54, 82, 90, 108, 126, 136, 164, 177
Nāgārjuna's commentary .. xvii, xviii, xxiii, 108
Nāgas 26, 99, 100, 120, 134
nirmāṇakāyas 69, 71, 91, 165
nirvana .. 25, 28, 46, 84-86, 124, 126, 127, 157-159, 163, 165, 175
noble one 35, 49, 52, 77, 82, 162, 167, 177

noble ones 52, 64, 149
non-dual bliss-emptiness wisdom 53
non-dualistic wisdom 169
non-virtue 76, 159
non-virtuous . 76, 77, 81, 87, 94, 104, 114, 129
non-virtuous karma 87, 129
not forgetting enlightenment mind 46, 88, 93, 102
object of prostration 62
obscuration .. 4, 5, 18, 128, 145, 169, 174
obstacles .. 87, 105, 106, 142, 145
ocean of aeons . 27, 29, 118, 119, 124, 131, 132, 135
ocean of aspects of the voice 24, 66
ocean of buddhas 27, 29, 56, 118, 119, 131
ocean of conduct 29, 131
ocean of dharmas ... 29, 130, 131
ocean of fields .. 27, 29, 118, 130
ocean of prayers 29, 131
ocean of sentient beings 29, 130
oceans of unending commendation 24, 66
ocean-like maṇḍala of Samantabhadra 55, 142
official translation of the prayer .... xvii, xxiii, 58
ointments 7, 24, 68
one instance of speech ... 99, 120
ones gone to bliss 24, 66, 67, 168
Orgyan Lord 106
origin of Samantabhadra's Prayer .... iii, xiii
ornament 5, 6, 10, 28, 86, 125, 169
Ornament of Manifest Realizations 86, 169
ornamentation 10, 28, 125

ornamentation of conquerors' fields 28
outflow 168
Padma Karpo Translation Committee . i, ii, xi, xxviii, 171, 173, 175-177
palms joined together ... 25, 84
papaṃ 161
pāramitās . 26, 51, 54, 60, 75, 98, 101, 110, 111, 128, 134, 153
passage into nirvana 25, 84
path of seeing .. 52, 64, 144, 151, 165
paths of accumulation and connection 52
Patrul Rinpoche .. 72, 74, 95, 96, 117
person who will make the prostration 60
phur ma 72
Piśhāci 49
poisons 76, 104, 168
prajñā 15, 19, 27, 29, 53, 61, 70, 86, 112, 116-118, 124, 127, 129, 131, 134, 143, 144, 153, 163, 168
Prajñāpāramitā sutras 15
Prajñāpāramitā teachings 61, 163
Prakrit 49
pratyekabuddhas ... 25, 80, 148
pratyekas 52, 63, 97, 116
prayer for accomplishing the antidote 47, 129
prayer for being ordained ... 46, 93, 96
prayer for conduct which is uncloaked or undefiled . 46, 88
prayer for enlightened activity 47, 88, 130
prayer for entering .. 47, 88, 118, 124
prayer for forces 47, 127
prayer for making effort at virtue 46, 93, 101
prayer for not forgetting enlightenment mind ... 46, 93
prayer for offering to the buddhas 46, 89
prayer for pure discipline 46, 93, 98
prayer for pure thought .. 46, 89
prayer for remembering the succession of lives .. 46, 93, 94
prayer for wearing armour 46, 109
prayer for wholly holding the holy dharma 46, 88, 115
prayer not to forget enlightenment mind 46, 93, 102
prayer of enlightenment 50, 138
prayer of excellent conduct .. 31, 43, 52, 142, 146, 147, 150, 151, 155
prayer to be able to teach dharma in various languages 46, 93, 99
prayer to be free from adverse circumstances 46, 93, 104
prayer to benefit sentient beings 46, 92
prayer to enter aeons ... 47, 122
prayer to enter going before the tathāgatas 47
prayer to enter their domain 47, 124
prayer to make offerings 46, 114
prayer to purify a buddha-field 46, 90
prayer to set sentient beings in benefit and ease 46, 108
prayer to train following the buddhas 47, 132

prayer to wholly fulfill the intent 89
prayers for enlightenment conduct 50
prayers for excellent conduct . 50
prayers of aspiration .. xi, xii, 87, 112
prayer's place in Tibetan Buddhist practice .... iii, xii
precious enlightenment mind 102, 104, 105
prior karmic debts 94
problems with the extracts . iii, xv
prostration ... 45, 53, 58, 60, 62, 66, 75, 146, 149
prostration through body . 45, 60
prostration through mind . 45, 62
prostration through speech 45, 66
pure levels 126
pure realm xi
purification of a field 92
Rāhula 63
rank of a buddha 61, 87, 92, 103, 104, 127, 130, 140
rational mind ... 28, 32, 64, 121, 124, 168
realization . 51, 83, 92, 115, 131, 158, 163, 169
referenced 49, 116, 128, 155, 169
referencing 73, 117, 169
refuge 78, 169
rejoicing .. 25, 45, 80-82, 85, 139
remember my births 26, 94
roots of merit ... 81, 82, 86, 139, 148, 153
Russian translations ...... viii, ix
saṃbhogakāyas 69, 71
sake of others .. 96, 105, 117, 153
samādhi . 16, 67, 73, 91, 95, 116-118, 124-126, 129, 134

samādhis 16, 27, 69, 73, 116, 117, 147, 152, 170
Samantabhadra ... i, iii-v, vii-xv, xvii, xix, xxii-xxiv, xxvi, 1, 3, 5-9, 12-17, 21-23, 30, 31, 33, 35, 37, 38, 41, 47, 48, 50-52, 55-57, 73, 83, 89, 111, 113, 116, 125, 128, 132-135, 142, 148-150, 155, 158, 159, 173, 177
primal guardian x
Samantabhadra's Prayer . i, iii-v, vii, viii, x-xiii, xv, xvii, xix, xxiv, xxvi, 33, 37, 38, 41, 113, 125, 158, 159, 173, 177
same lot 46, 88, 111
samsara .... xi, 18, 64, 76, 77, 85, 87, 106, 107, 116, 117, 124, 129, 131, 139, 146, 149, 151, 153, 157-159, 162, 163, 165, 167, 169-171, 174
samsaric mind 168, 171
Sanskrit .... iv, xvi-xix, xxii, xxiv, xxviii, 3, 32, 38, 49, 51, 56, 59, 67, 101, 115, 117, 119, 145, 157-162, 164-171, 173, 174
Sanskrit texts 3
satva and sattva 159, 170
sentient beings .... xii, 4-6, 8-15, 17, 19-23, 25, 29, 31, 32, 46, 48, 50, 60, 62, 64, 79, 83, 86, 88, 89, 92, 93, 95, 97, 100, 103, 104, 107-110, 112, 114-116, 120, 121, 124, 127, 128, 130, 131, 135, 137-139, 145-147, 149-157, 161, 163-167, 170, 174
seven limbs of accumulation . 45, 58
seven major editions of *The Translated Word* ...... xxii, 173

shining forth 170
six pāramitās 51, 60, 75, 98,
    101, 110, 111, 128, 134
six qualities of "goodness" ... 53
sixty branches of voice 120
small cymbals 24, 68, 70
son of the gods 130
special intention . 9, 86, 109, 171
spiritual friends . 3, 4, 19, 21, 32,
    38, 83, 84, 88, 93, 113
sprout of enlightenment mind 104
stupa containing the Buddha's
    relics 62
Subhuti 38
succession of lives ... 46, 93, 94
Sudhana ... iv, xiii, xiv, xxii, xxiii,
    xxvi, 1, 3, 6, 8, 12, 15-17, 21, 51,
    55-57, 142
suffering of the bad migrations
    .... 26, 108
Sukhāvatī ..... x, xi, 31, 91, 125,
    131, 134, 141, 150, 152, 154,
    156
Sukhāvatī Prayer .... x, xi
superfactual 73, 86, 98, 117,
    148, 158, 162, 163, 171, 172
superfactual enlightenment mind
    158
superfactual truth 148, 162,
    163, 171, 172
superfactual truth enlightenment
    mind 162, 172
superfice 172
superficies 65, 121, 172
superior merits 30, 139, 154
supplication 78, 83-85, 126
supports for study .. iv, xi, xxviii,
    175
supreme of lamps 70
supreme oil lamps 24, 68

supreme parasols 24, 68
supreme scents 24, 68
Surendrabodhi 32, 35, 38
surpassable offering 45, 68
sustained in goodness .. 30, 141
sutra . ii, iv, v, vii, viii, xi, xiii, xiv,
    xvii, xxii-xxvi, xxviii, xxix, 1, 3, 15,
    32, 35, 38, 39, 50, 53, 55, 59, 74,
    79, 81, 92, 100, 103, 111, 113,
    143, 144, 157, 171, 173, 177
Sutra of the Householder Uncouth
    177
Sutra of the Recollection of the Noble
    Three Jewels 53, 171, 177
syntax . xvi, xvii, xix, xxi, xxiv, 119
Tāranātha .... xviii, 54
tathāgata
    explanation 59
ten strengths 60, 67, 123
Tenpa'i Wangchuk ..... i, iv, xii,
    xiii, xx, xxi, xxvi, 41-43, 55, 59,
    74, 85
Tenpa'i Wangchuk's commentary
    55
tenth bodhisatva level .... x, xiv,
    xxiv
tīrthika 31, 145, 173
the actual prayer 46, 88
the actual topics of the text 45, 58
the best of excellent displays
    .... 24, 68, 72
the bodhisatva path x
the buddhas of the future . 59, 90
the buddhas of the past 59
the end of the prayer xii, 47, 137
the excellent thought 51, 60,
    75, 92, 94, 110, 145
the five immediates . 31, 76, 142,
    143, 150
the four forces of antidote 77, 143

INDEX

the four māras 62, 152
the four things of gathering . . 98
the importance of
    Samantabhadra's Prayer . . iii, x
the ocean-like field realms of
    Samantabhadra 56
the origin of Samantabhadra's
    Prayer . . . . iii, xiii
the prayer is an extract . . . . iii, xiv
the prayer itself 39
the prayer's advantages . . 47, 138
the prefatory topics 45, 49
the realm of knowables 65
the seven limbs 45, 58
The Sutra of Giving Advice to the
    King 103
the teacher of the present . . . 59
the three dharma robes 71
the three types of faith 60
The Translated Treatises 173
The Translated Word . . . . xxii-xxv,
    3, 125, 173
the undefiled state 25, 82
the unsurpassed wheel . . . 25, 82,
    83
third order thousandfold world
    system 172
thirteen benefits 140
thirty-seven dharmas 67
this king of dedications . . 30, 139
thoroughly virtuous excellent
    conduct 30, 134
three bad migrations . . 109, 154,
    156
Three Hundred 49, 100
Three Jewels . . . 53, 78, 87, 106,
    109, 169, 171, 177
three poisons 76, 104, 168
three secrets . . . 67, 68, 136, 170,
    172
three types of faith 60
three Vehicles 81, 109, 147,
    164, 172
three worlds 31, 79, 146
Tibetan arrangement xv
Tibetan commentaries . . . iii, vii,
    viii, xvii-xxi, xxiv, xxv, 39
Tibetan experts . . . . ix, xviii, 51,
    111, 170
Tibetan explanations of the prayer
    vii
title . . . . vii, 45, 49-51, 164
Tobbar Ozer 54
topics . . xxviii, 45, 47, 49, 52, 58,
    88, 102, 131, 132, 136, 137
transformations . . 15, 17, 20, 23,
    30, 136
transgressions of the bodhisatva
    trainings 76
transgressions of the vidyādhara
    mantra samayas 76
transgressions of the vows . . . 76
transgressions of the vows of
    personal emancipation 76
translator's prostration . . . 45, 53
transmission . . . . ix, xxi
true existence 64
truly complete buddha . . 59, 150,
    153, 158, 161, 164
trusting faith 75
turn the wheel of dharma . . . 11,
    120, 121, 126, 147
twenty-one good qualities 67
types of offering 72
Śākyamitra . . . . xvi, 54
Śākyamuni Buddha . . . x, xi, 68,
    95, 148
Śāntideva . . . . x-xii, 94, 97, 134,
    138, 145
Śāriputra 95, 112

śhrāvaka . 52, 63, 80, 97, 98, 116, 148
uncorrupted and faultless   26, 98
under the control of not knowing
.... 31, 142
unending . 24, 27, 28, 47, 53, 56, 66, 88, 92, 115-117, 120, 121, 138, 143, 171, 177
unending store .. 27, 47, 88, 116, 117
Unending Torment 143
unending voices of speech 28, 121
unfathomable 56, 62, 66, 73, 75, 89, 109, 114, 150, 162
universes .. xi, 59, 60, 62, 80, 114, 125, 151
unsatisfactoriness ... 32, 60, 138, 154, 169, 174
unsurpassable offering ... 45, 73
unsurpassed offering 74
unsurpassed offerings .. 74, 115
un-outflowed .. 60, 67, 123, 168, 173
urging 25, 45, 82, 85, 156
utterly express 19
utterly prostrate 24, 60, 62
Vairochana ... xxiv, 9, 14, 16, 56, 89, 95, 155
Vajra Vehicle 163, 164, 173
Vajrasatva 71, 89, 170
Vasubhandu xvi
viewing the fields 47, 118
virtuous karma 87, 94, 129
voice 23, 24, 28, 66, 120, 121, 149
vows of personal emancipation
.... 76, 129
Western translators 170
wheel of dharma 11, 49, 95, 118, 120-122, 126, 147
wholly holding the holy dharma
.... 46, 88, 115
wisdom .. 8, 9, 15, 16, 18, 19, 21, 29, 31, 53, 64, 67, 77, 117, 118, 121, 124, 127, 128, 130, 131, 144, 148, 159, 167-169, 171, 173, 174, 177
wisdom mind 121, 171
wish-fulfilling jewel ... 113, 141
world realms ... 7-9, 12-14, 16, 21-23, 38, 56, 58, 59, 63, 64, 67, 77, 85, 89, 91, 92, 114, 118, 119, 122, 126, 139, 141, 153
worlds of the ten directions .. 23, 25, 82, 83, 89
yakṣhas 120
Yeshe De .. vi, xvii, xx, xxiii, xxiv, 32, 35, 38, 58, 74, 113
Yeshe De's commentary .... viii, xviii, xxiv, 74
Yeshe De's Tibetan commentary
.... vii
Zur Phud Ngapa 54

www.ingramcontent.com/pod-product-compliance
Lightning Source LLC
Chambersburg PA
CBHW022007160426
43197CB00007B/311